Vegetarian Times LOW-FAT & *Fast*

Vegetarian Times
Low-Fat & Fast

From the Editors of
Vegetarian Times magazine

Macmillan • USA

MACMILLAN

A Simon & Schuster Macmillan Company
1633 Broadway
New York, NY 10019-6785

Library of Congress Cataloging-in-Publication Data
Vegetarian times low-fat & fast / by the editors of Vegetarian times magazine
p. cm.
Includes index.
ISBN: 0-02-861588-3 (alk. paper)
1. Vegetarian cookery. 2. Low-fat diet—Recipes. 3. Quick and easy cookery.
I. Vegetarian times.
TX837.V4273 1997   96-43586
641.5'636—dc20   CIP

Design by Amy Peppler Adams—designLab, Seattle

Manufactured in the United States of America

10 9 8 7 6 5 4 3 2

Contents

Acknowledgments

The editors of *Vegetarian Times* would like to thank the many recipe developers who have contributed to *Vegetarian Times* over the years, and whose works grace these pages, particularly the kitchens of Cowles Creative Publishing. Our sincere and heartfelt thanks and appreciation go to test kitchen supervisor Ellen Boeke and staff Elizabeth Emmons and Nancy Johnson for their enthusiasm and dedication to this project.

Thanks also to Justin Schwartz at Macmillan Publishing for the opportunity to put this cookbook series together. As always, working with him is a pleasure.

Personal thanks go to Toni Apgar, editorial director of *Vegetarian Times*, for her trust in me and confidence in my abilities; and to Terry Christofferson, editorial assistant, for her software wizardry and her renowned cheerful, helpful demeanor.

—Carol Wiley Lorente
Special Projects Editor
Vegetarian Times

Introduction

L ow-fat cooking has never been more popular. More than ever, people recognize that eating a diet containing less fat and more complex carbohydrates goes a long way toward the prevention of heart disease, diabetes, obesity, high cholesterol, high blood pressure, and the other illnesses that ravage Americans.

But recipes for low-fat dishes aren't enough anymore: We know you're busy. You want healthful meals, but you want convenience too. And we know that if you're like more and more Americans, you want those meals to be meatless. How do we know?

Vegetarian Times magazine has been the authority on vegetarianism since its beginnings in 1974. Since instituting the "Low-Fat and Fast" column in *Vegetarian Times* magazine eight years ago, it has become the most well-read section of our magazine. It's only natural then that we follow it with a cookbook series based on the same premise: tasty, low-fat, vegetarian meals in about thirty minutes or less.

Vegetarian Times Low-Fat & Fast is a cookbook series designed for the way health-minded Americans like you want to eat. Each volume will contain 150 to 200 delicious recipes—appetizers and snacks, main dishes, side dishes, and desserts—that are guaranteed to satisfy your need for healthful cooking and your desire to get food on the table fast.

And whether you're seeking meatless meals for reasons of health, animal rights, environment, or religion, you'll find plenty to like in *Vegetarian Times Low-Fat & Fast*. Of the 175 recipes in this first volume, 94 of the recipes are vegan, calling for no animal-derived foods, and 31 others can be made vegan by using the vegan alternatives listed in the recipe. Other recipes also can be made vegan by substituting your favorite replacement products for dairy and eggs.

HOW TO COOK LOW FAT

Eating a low-fat diet—and cooking low-fat meals—isn't as difficult as you might think. Our advice has always been to base your meals and snacks on whole grains, beans, fruits, and vegetables; they're naturally low in fat and calories, and they contain all of the vitamins, minerals, and fiber you need. If you eat eggs, do so only occasionally; they're high in fat and cholesterol. If you eat dairy products, use them sparingly, or switch to low-fat or nonfat varieties.

Use the following tips to help you switch to low-fat cooking:

— Food must taste great. You don't ever have to settle for boring, bland-tasting food, even if it *is* good for you. Fat is a flavor enhancer, so when you cut the fat, you have to up the flavor in other ways. Learn to use fresh herbs, spices, and other flavorings—mustards, vinegars, juices and citrus peels, aromatic fruits and vegetables, chutneys, and so on.

— Use naturally low-fat cooking techniques, such as steaming, broiling, baking, and sautéing.

— Use oils sparingly. Sauté in water, vegetable broth, vegetable or fruit juices, or wine.

— Use high-quality ingredients. It makes more sense to use a little of a good-quality, full-flavored food than a large amount of a poor-quality, reduced-fat product. For example, just one tablespoon of freshly grated Asiago cheese over a dish of hot pasta adds more flavor and aroma than $1/4$ cup of a low-quality Parmesan cheese from a box. In the same vein, shop and cook seasonally; the flavors that burst from fresh produce will enable you to cut way down on fat and still retain flavor.

— In baking, substitute up to half of the fat called for in the recipe with pureed fruit, such as applesauce or prunes, or with nonfat plain yogurt.

— In cooking, experiment with your favorite nonfat, low-fat, or vegetarian foods for the ingredients called for in the recipe. For example, when a recipe calls for mayonnaise, substitute low-fat regular mayonnaise or tofu mayonnaise (available in natural food stores). When a recipe calls for eggs, experiment with liquid egg substitutes (they are egg-based, however, and contain preservatives) or Egg Replacer, a natural, nonfat, egg-free product found in natural food stores. (A little tofu or mashed banana also will hold baked goods together.)

- A huge portion of the fat in the diets of American women comes from salad dressing. Make your own fat-free dressings with pureed vegetables, fruit or vegetable juices, vinegar, mustard, or fat-free mayonnaise.

- To thicken soups without cream, remove one or two cups of the cooked vegetables from the soup, puree, and stir back into the pot. Instant mashed potato flakes and rolled oats added to the soup will thicken it as well.

- Fried equals fat. Make it a habit to skip fried foods. Instead, try baking them. For french fries, for example, try slicing potatoes thin, spraying them lightly with nonstick cooking spray, adding fresh herbs and spices to taste, and baking them on nonstick baking sheets until golden brown.

- Remember: Healthful eating doesn't have to mean radical, dramatic changes in your family's meal plans. Start out by preparing "slimmed-down" versions of familiar favorites: Try spaghetti with a marinara sauce that's heavy on the fresh tomatoes and spices and light on the oil, for example. Or prepare your favorite tacos with crispy shells, nonfat refried beans, vegetables, and lots of salsa and fresh cilantro.

- Shop the perimeter of the supermarket. That's where you'll find the produce, and most of the whole grain breads and other fresh, whole foods. As you shop, remember that just because a food is low in fat or fat free doesn't mean it's good for you! There is a multitude of low-fat and nonfat processed foods on the market these days. Eating an entire bag of nonfat cookies or low-fat potato chips is no more healthful than eating an entire bag of the high-octane variety. Of course you aren't getting all of the fat of the regular kinds, but you're still eating an abundance of unnecessary and perhaps harmful calories, sugar, sodium, and chemical "nonfoods" that are taking the place of whole foods. Stick to whole grains, beans, fruits, and vegetables, and you'll be sure to be eating a healthful diet. It's that easy.

FAST FOOD

All of the recipes in *Vegetarian Times Low-Fat & Fast* take around thirty minutes or less to prepare. But getting your own favorite meals on the table also can be easier when you know a few tricks. Most of it boils down to planning and completing tasks as the food cooks. Here are some tips for quick cooking:

- Set out all ingredients and utensils you'll need before you begin cooking, and mentally organize the preparation so you can "dove-tail" steps. For example, while the pasta is cooking, chop the garlic and tomatoes for the sauce. (We've written the recipes in this cookbook in such a manner to help you do this.)

- Organize and equip your kitchen to your advantage. Keep frequently used utensils, such as wooden spoons, rubber scrapers, spatulas, and whisks in a container or drawer next to the stove; keep pots, pans, mixing bowls, and measuring cups nearby. And return these items to the same places so you won't have to hunt for them next time.

- Wholesome, nutritious foods do come in convenient, prepared forms— use them! Frozen vegetables, canned beans, bagged, cut-up and shredded produce, fresh pastas, canned vegetable broths, and other prepared foods are wholesome and of good quality and save time.

- Along that line, also try quick-cooking grains. Whole-food, quick-cooking versions of rice and barley are available. Other grains, such as bulgur, quinoa, and couscous, are naturally quick cooking.

- There are simple ways to speed the actual heating and cooking of foods. Smaller and thinner cuts of vegetables cook more quickly than thick ones. Wide-diameter skillets and pots speed up heating and simmering.

- If you're a weekend cook, make a point to cook twice as much as you need and freeze or refrigerate the leftovers to eat later in the week. This suggestion also works well for parts of the meal other than the main dish. It's easy to whip up fried rice, for instance, when the rice is already cooked and waiting in the refrigerator.

- If your food processor and slow cooker have been out of sight and out of mind lately, move them out of the cupboard and onto the countertop, where they'll remind you to use them. The food processor, of course, will make fast work of shredding and chopping. And the slow cooker, well, yes, it takes all day to cook a meal, but you can't beat it for convenience: Just throw in the ingredients, turn it on, and go. Dinner is ready when you get home.

ABOUT OUR RECIPES

After each recipe, we provide nutritional information that lists the amount of calories, protein, fat, carbohydrates, cholesterol, sodium, and fiber per serving. When a choice of ingredients is given (as in "skim milk or soy milk"), the analysis reflects the first ingredient listed (skim milk). When there is a range of servings (as in "1 to 2 tablespoons olive oil"), the analysis reflects the first number listed (1 tablespoon). When an ingredient is listed as optional, it is not included in the nutritional analysis.

We do not list the percentage of calories from fat per serving because we believe it is misleading. The percent of fat in a given recipe is less important than the percent of fat eaten in an entire day. The bulk of research indicates that fat intake must be less than 25 percent of calories to prevent disease and to promote health. So if you eat 2,000 calories per day, you can eat 55 grams of fat per day and maintain a diet that obtains 25 percent of calories from fat. You could easily find enough recipes in *Vegetarian Times Low-Fat & Fast* to prepare three meals a day and still remain at or below 55 grams of fat per day.

Where appropriate, we also give variations and helpful hints after recipes. Variations suggest other ways of preparing the recipe; helpful hints discuss advance preparation, list how-to's, define terms and ingredients, and tell you where to buy them.

We think you'll find this first volume of *Vegetarian Times Low-Fat & Fast* a practical guide to cooking fast and healthful vegetarian meals. Happy cooking.

CHAPTER 1

Appetizers and Snacks

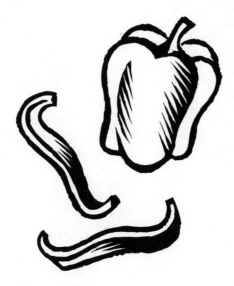

Easy Low-Fat Garlic Bread

½ cup nonfat Italian dressing
2 or more cloves garlic, minced
½ teaspoon paprika
One 1-pound loaf whole wheat
    bread, preferably French-
    style
Dried parsley flakes (optional)

Preheat broiler.

In a small mixing bowl, combine dressing, garlic, and paprika. Whisk until smooth.

Cut bread into slices (½-inch thick for regular bread and 1-inch thick for French). Brush dressing mixture evenly on one side of bread slices. Sprinkle with parsley flakes, if desired.

Arrange slices on a baking sheet and place under broiler with surface of slices 4 inches from heat. Broil until light golden brown, about 3 minutes, watching carefully so bread does not burn.

Makes 12 servings

VARIATION

Sprinkle garlic bread with chopped fresh basil to taste just before serving.

Per Serving:
147 Calories; 5g Protein; 2g Fat;
26g Carbohydrates; 0 Cholesterol;
306mg Sodium; 0 Fiber.

Chèvre and Sun-Dried Tomato Pâté

¼ cup low-fat cottage cheese,
   drained
One 3-ounce jar oil-packed sun-
   dried tomatoes, drained
   and chopped
2 ounces chèvre (goat cheese)
⅛ teaspoon dried thyme leaves
8 large slices French or Italian
   bread
2 teaspoons finely chopped
   fresh parsley

In a food processor or blender, process cottage cheese until smooth. In a medium mixing bowl, combine pureed cottage cheese, tomatoes, chèvre, and thyme; mix well.

Lightly toast bread and spread cheese mixture evenly over slices. Top with parsley.

Makes 8 servings

Per Serving:
112 Calories; 4g Protein; 3g Fat; 14g Carbohydrates; 7mg Cholesterol; 151mg Sodium; 1g Fiber.

Crostini with Olive Paste and Sliced Tomatoes

1 cup pitted black or kalamata
    olives
2 tablespoons finely chopped
    shallot or onion
2 tablespoons capers, rinsed
    (optional)
2 tablespoons olive oil
¼ teaspoon dried thyme leaves
2 to 3 teaspoons lemon juice or
    red wine vinegar
16 slices French bread, cut ¼-
    inch thick
1 to 2 cloves garlic, cut in half
16 small plum or cherry toma-
    toes, sliced
Fresh basil leaves
Freshly ground black pepper
    to taste

In a food processor, combine olives, shallot or onion, capers if desired, oil, and thyme. Process to desired texture. Stir in lemon juice or vinegar. Set mixture aside.

Toast bread lightly and immediately rub one side of each slice with cut side of garlic clove. Spread olive paste evenly on toast slices. Top with a slice or two of tomato. Garnish with basil leaves. Season with pepper to taste.

Makes 16 appetizers; 8 servings

VARIATION

*Instead of tomatoes, top crostini
with roasted peppers or
pickled onions.*

Per Serving:
194 Calories; 6g Protein; 6g Fat;
30g Carbohydrates; 0 Cholesterol;
332mg Sodium; 2g Fiber.

Mango Chutney

Serve this chutney on bread or atop crackers with melted cheese. It's also a tasty condiment for any Indian or curry-flavored dish.

1 ripe mango, peeled and diced (about 1½ cups)
½ cup sugar
¼ cup finely chopped red onion
2 tablespoons apple cider vinegar
2 tablespoons finely chopped green bell pepper
1 tablespoon grated fresh ginger root
¼ teaspoon ground cloves
Freshly ground black pepper to taste

In a 2-quart saucepan, combine all ingredients. Cook over medium heat, stirring occasionally, until mango is soft and mixture is thickened, about 10 to 15 minutes.

Cool slightly. Cover and chill. (To cool quickly, spread chutney in a shallow dish and place in freezer, stirring occasionally, until chilled.) Serve chutney with cheese or on bread.

Makes 1 cup; 8 servings

Per Serving:
70 Calories; 0 Protein; 0 Fat;
18g Carbohydrates; 0 Cholesterol;
2mg Sodium; 0 Fiber.

Herbed White Bean Puree

This smooth creamy puree resembles herbed cheese spread in texture and flavor. It's great with crackers or raw vegetables or as a sandwich spread. You can make it as flavorful as you want to by the inclusion or omission of optional ingredients.

½ cup finely chopped shallots or scallions
2 to 3 cloves garlic, chopped
2 cups cooked or canned great northern or navy beans, rinsed and drained
2 tablespoons finely chopped fresh parsley or chives (optional)
1 tablespoon capers, rinsed and drained, or 1 to 2 teaspoons prepared stone-ground mustard (optional)
1 tablespoon fresh lemon juice or white wine vinegar
1 tablespoon tahini (see Helpful Hint) or olive oil (optional)
½ teaspoon dried basil
½ teaspoon dried thyme
½ teaspoon dill
½ teaspoon dried tarragon
½ teaspoon salt
¼ teaspoon white pepper
¼ teaspoon ground nutmeg
Dash hot pepper sauce (optional)
Watercress, fresh herbs, lemon slices, or olives for garnish

In a food processor or blender, process shallots or scallions and garlic until very finely chopped. Add remaining ingredients except hot pepper sauce and garnishes. Process until smooth.

Adjust seasonings to taste, adding hot pepper sauce and additional lemon juice or vinegar, if desired.

Transfer to a serving dish and add garnishes. Serve with whole grain crackers, breadsticks, or fresh vegetables.

Makes about 2 cups; eight ¼-cup servings

Helpful Hint

Tahini (or sesame paste) is a thick, smooth paste made of ground sesame seeds. It has a taste and aroma reminiscent of peanut butter. Tahini is sold in cans and jars in supermarkets, natural food stores, and in Middle Eastern markets.

Per Serving:
62 Calories; 4g Protein; <1g Fat; 12g Carbohydrates; 0 Cholesterol; 136mg Sodium; 3g Fiber.

Roasted Red Bell Pepper Dip

This simple low-fat dip capitalizes on the unique flavor of roasted red bell pepper. Use jarred peppers for faster preparation.

1 red bell pepper, roasted,
    peeled and chopped, or ½
    cup jarred roasted red bell
    pepper, drained and
    chopped
2 tablespoons fresh lemon juice
2 tablespoons mayonnaise
1 tablespoon olive oil
1½ cups crumbled firm tofu
Salt and freshly ground black
    pepper to taste

In a food processor or blender, combine bell pepper, lemon juice, mayonnaise, and oil. Process until smooth. Add tofu, salt, and pepper. Process until smooth, scraping sides of bowl, if necessary. Serve dip with whole grain crackers, toasted Italian bread, breadsticks, or raw vegetables.

**Makes about 2 cups;
16 servings**

VARIATIONS

Add a dash of hot pepper sauce, or a clove or two of minced garlic.

Substitute red wine vinegar for the lemon juice.

Serve in hollowed-out green bell peppers.

Helpful Hint

To roast a pepper, place it under a broiler 3 to 4 inches from heat. Turn pepper frequently until skin is blackened, about 5 minutes. Seal pepper in a plastic or paper bag and let it steam for 10 minutes. Peel pepper, remove seeds, and chop.

Per Serving:
38 Calories; 2g Protein; 4g Fat;
2g Carbohydrates; <1 Cholesterol;
52mg Sodium; <1 Fiber.

Black and Gold Cucumber Logs

2 medium cucumbers
One 15-ounce can garbanzo
**   beans (chickpeas), rinsed**
**   and drained**
⅓ cup fresh lemon juice
1 tablespoon olive oil
1 tablespoon water
1 clove garlic, minced
1½ teaspoons salt
¼ cup finely chopped black
**   olives**

Remove lengthwise strips of peel from cucumbers to create stripes. Cut off ends of cucumbers. Cut each cucumber into 6 rounds and set them on their ends. With a melon baller or spoon, make a well in the center of each round. Set aside.

In a food processor or blender, combine beans, lemon juice, oil, water, garlic, and salt. Process until smooth, adding water if necessary for a smooth puree.

Stir in olives. Spoon puree evenly into hollowed-out cucumber rounds.

Makes 12 servings

VARIATION

Use kalamata olives instead of black olives for a more pungent flavor.

Helpful Hint

Filling can be made several days before cucumber rounds need to be filled. Assemble rounds just before serving.

Per Serving:
82 Calories; 3g Protein; 2g Fat; 12g Carbohydrates; 0 Cholesterol; 291mg Sodium; 3g Fiber.

Pears with Lime-Peanut Chutney

These simple appetizers have an intriguing blend of flavors that are sweet, sour, and spicy. The chutney can be prepared ahead of time.

¼ to ½ **cup dry-roasted peanuts, finely chopped**
2 tablespoons packed brown sugar
1 to 2 tablespoons fresh lime juice, plus extra juice to keep pears from browning
Zest from 1 lime (see Helpful Hint)
1 clove garlic, minced
1 teaspoon soy sauce
¼ **teaspoon red pepper flakes**
3 medium or 6 small pears
Fresh mint leaves for garnish

To prepare chutney, in a small bowl, combine peanuts, sugar, lime juice, zest, garlic, soy sauce, and red pepper flakes. Set aside.

Cut each pear lengthwise into quarters. (If using very small pears, cut into halves.) Remove and discard cores. Using a melon baller or grapefruit spoon, make a well in the center of each quarter. Sprinkle cut surfaces of pear lightly with extra lime juice to prevent browning.

Spoon chutney evenly into pear quarters. Garnish with mint sprigs.

Makes 12 appetizers; 6 servings

Helpful Hint

Zest is the outermost peel of citrus fruit, used as seasoning. It can be made fresh, by grating the rind of the citrus fruit, but it also is available in bottles in the spice aisle of the supermarket.

Per Serving:
104 Calories; 2g Protein; 4g Fat; 14g Carbohydrates; 0 Cholesterol; 52mg Sodium; 2g Fiber.

Cream Cheese Roll-Ups

**2 ounces Neufchâtel cheese or
cream cheese, softened**
3 tablespoons mayonnaise
3 tablespoons Dijon mustard
**4 large chapatis (see Helpful
Hint) or flour tortillas**
1 cup thinly sliced cucumbers
1 cup thinly sliced tomatoes
1 cup shredded lettuce
**½ teaspoon salt or herbal salt
substitute (optional)**

In a small bowl, mash together
cheese, mayonnaise, and mustard.
Spread a strip of cheese mixture
across the center of one chapati or
tortilla. Arrange cucumbers,
tomatoes, and lettuce in rows over
cheese mixture, and sprinkle with
salt or salt substitute, if desired.

Roll bread up tightly, sealing
end with a dab of cheese mixture.
Repeat with remaining chapatis or
tortillas and cheese mixture.

Place rolls seam-side down on a
cutting surface and slice crosswise
into quarters. If necessary, secure
roll-ups with toothpicks.

Makes 16 servings

VARIATION

*Slice into smaller pieces and serve
cut-side up.*

Helpful Hint

*Chapatis are unleavened breads
from India similar to tortillas,
made from a simple mixture of
whole wheat flour and water.*

Per Serving:
70 Calories; 2g Protein; 5g Fat;
6g Carbohydrates; 4mg Cholesterol; 153mg Sodium; 1g Fiber.

Tortellini Skewers with Garlic-Parmesan Sauce

These skewered appetizers go together in a flash, making good use of fresh tortellini.

72 fresh cheese tortellini (about 25 ounces)
Twenty-four 4-inch wooden skewers
6 tablespoons finely chopped fresh parsley
½ cup olive oil
½ cup freshly grated Parmesan cheese
⅓ cup fresh lemon juice
3 cloves garlic, minced
Salt and freshly ground black pepper to taste

Prepare the tortellini according to package directions. Rinse with cold water and drain.

Thread 3 tortellini on each skewer. Arrange skewers on a platter and sprinkle with 2 tablespoons parsley.

In a small bowl, whisk together 4 tablespoons parsley, oil, cheese, lemon juice, garlic, salt, and pepper. (If desired, process mixture in a blender for 1 minute.) Brush sauce on tortellini and serve. Reserve any remaining sauce for dipping when skewers are served.

Makes 24 skewers

VARIATIONS

For a more colorful presentation, use tomato, spinach, or herb tortellini.

Per Skewer:
176 Calories; 8g Protein; 7g Fat; 21g Carbohydrates; 28mg Cholesterol; 222mg Sodium; <1g Fiber.

Lone Star "Caviar"

2 medium tomatoes, seeded
  and chopped (2 cups)
One 15-ounce can black-eyed
  peas, rinsed and drained
1 medium green bell pepper,
  seeded and chopped (about
  1⅓ cups)
½ cup sliced scallions
2 tablespoons fresh lemon or
  lime juice
1 to 2 fresh jalapeño peppers,
  seeded and finely chopped
2 cloves garlic, minced
1 teaspoon chili powder
½ teaspoon ground cumin
½ teaspoon salt
Fresh cilantro or parsley as
  garnish

In a medium bowl, combine all ingredients except cilantro or parsley. Let stand at room temperature for 10 minutes, stirring occasionally. Transfer to a serving bowl. Garnish with cilantro or parsley. Serve with baked tortilla chips or corn chips.

Makes 5 cups; 20 servings

Per Serving:
22 Calories; 1g Protein; <1g Fat;
4g Carbohydrates; 0 Cholesterol;
96mg Sodium; 1g Fiber.

Creamy Salsa Dip

½ cup nonfat plain yogurt
   cheese (see Helpful Hint)
½ cup chunky salsa, drained
1 to 2 tablespoons skim milk
1 tablespoon fresh lime juice
¼ teaspoon ground cumin
Sliced scallions or chopped
   fresh chives as garnish

In a small bowl, combine yogurt cheese, salsa, milk, lime juice, and cumin. (Use more or less milk depending on desired thickness of dip.) Transfer dip to a serving dish. Garnish with scallions or chives.

Makes 1 cup

Helpful Hint

To make yogurt cheese, spoon yogurt into a mesh strainer or colander that has been lined with paper towels or cheesecloth. Place over a bowl and cover with plastic wrap. Let drain overnight in refrigerator; store in an airtight container. (1 cup yogurt makes about ⅔ cup yogurt cheese.)

Per Tablespoon:
12 Calories; 1g Protein; 0 Fat; 2g Carbohydrates; <1mg Cholesterol; 98mg Sodium; <1g Fiber.

Hummus

This traditional Middle Eastern dip made from mashed garbanzo beans is usually served with pieces of pita bread and raw vegetables. It also makes a terrific sandwich filler with plain or roasted vegetables.

Two 15-ounce cans garbanzo beans (chickpeas), rinsed and drained
¼ cup fresh lemon juice
2 tablespoons chopped fresh parsley
2 tablespoons water
1 tablespoon olive oil or sesame oil
1 to 2 cloves garlic, minced
¼ teaspoon cayenne pepper
Whole wheat pita bread, cut into wedges, or raw vegetables (optional)

Combine all ingredients except pita or raw vegetables in a food processor or blender. Process until smooth, scraping sides of bowl as necessary. If a thinner dip is desired, add more water. Serve hummus with pita wedges or raw vegetables.

Makes 2½ cups; 10 servings

Per Serving:
116 Calories; 4g Protein; 4g Fat; 20g Carbohydrates; 0 Cholesterol; 252mg Sodium; 4g Fiber.

Caponata

1 medium eggplant, cut into
½-inch slices
1 tablespoon olive oil or garlic-
flavored oil
¼ cup pine nuts
¼ cup balsamic vinegar or red
wine vinegar
1 small onion, chopped (about
½ cup)
⅓ cup sliced celery
One 14½-ounce can diced
tomatoes, drained
¼ cup sliced black olives
1 tablespoon capers, drained
(see Helpful Hint)
1 teaspoon dried oregano
leaves
¼ teaspoon freshly ground
black pepper
Italian bread, sliced and
toasted, or whole grain
crackers (optional)
Freshly grated Parmesan
cheese (optional)

Preheat broiler. Brush both sides of
eggplant slices evenly with oil.
Arrange eggplant on baking sheet.
Broil 5 inches from heat until
eggplant is tender and browned,
about 15 minutes, turning once.
Chop eggplant; set aside.

Meanwhile, place pine nuts in a
small dry skillet over medium-low
heat. Cook, shaking pan occasionally, until nuts are lightly
browned, about 5 minutes.

Heat vinegar in a medium nonstick skillet over medium heat.
Add onion and celery. Sauté until
tender, about 5 minutes. Stir in
remaining ingredients. Simmer for
2 minutes, stirring occasionally.
Stir in eggplant and pine nuts.
Remove from heat; cool slightly,
stirring occasionally.

Serve caponata on toasted Italian
bread or whole grain crackers
topped with Parmesan, if desired.

Makes 4½ cups

VARIATION

*Cut fresh zucchini into rounds and
hollow them out as in Black and
Gold Cucumber Logs, page 8. Fill
hollowed-out rounds with
Caponata.*

Helpful Hint

*Capers are the flower buds of a
Mediterranean bush that are
pickled or dried and used as a
condiment. They are sold in small
jars and bags in the supermarket.
Look for them in the olive or pickles
section of the supermarket.*

Per Tablespoon:
10 Calories; <1g Protein; <1g Fat;
1g Carbohydrates; 0 Cholesterol;
26mg Sodium; <1g Fiber.

Fruity Soy Shakes

The goodness of soy in a milkshake!
These shakes also make a great breakfast.

1 cup vanilla soy milk, chilled
5 ounces (half of a 10½-ounce
  package) soft silken tofu,
  chilled and cubed
2 cups fresh or frozen fruit (one
  or more varieties of your
  choice)
1 to 2 tablespoons honey or rice
  syrup (see Helpful Hint)
½ teaspoon vanilla extract

Combine all ingredients in a
blender. Process until smooth.

Makes 2 shakes; 2 servings

VARIATIONS

Peanut Butter-Banana Shake:
Prepare as directed above, substi-
tuting 1 cup sliced bananas (about 2
medium) for 2 cups fruit. Reduce
honey or rice syrup to 1 tablespoon,
omit vanilla and add 3 tablespoons
natural peanut butter.

Peanut Butter-Chocolate Shake:
Prepare as directed above, omitting
fruit and vanilla. Add ¼ cup
natural peanut butter and 2
tablespoons unsweetened cocoa.
Increase honey or rice syrup to 3
tablespoons.

Helpful Hint

Rice syrup is a liquid sweetener
made from brown rice. Its mild
flavor makes it perfect when you
want to avoid the sharp sweetness
of white sugar or honey. It is sold in
natural food stores.

Per Shake:
157 Calories; 8g Protein; 5g Fat;
24g Carbohydrates; 0 Cholesterol;
21mg Sodium; 5g Fiber.

Bagel Chips

SEASONING MIX:

2 teaspoons salt
1 teaspoon onion powder
1 teaspoon garlic powder
½ teaspoon white pepper
½ teaspoon paprika

CHIPS:

6 plain bagels
Nonstick cooking spray

Preheat oven to 400°F.

In a small bowl, combine seasoning mix ingredients. Set aside.

Cut each bagel crosswise into 4 slices approximately ¼ inch thick. Spray both sides of slices with nonstick cooking spray. Sprinkle both sides evenly with seasoning mix.

Spray 2 baking sheets with nonstick cooking spray. Arrange bagel slices in a single layer on baking sheets. Bake until bagel slices are golden and crispy, about 10 minutes, turning once. Use bagel chips as you would crackers or chips.

Makes 24 chips; 6 servings

Per Serving:
300 Calories; 12g Protein; 2g Fat; 60g Carbohydrates; 0 Cholesterol; 1,632mg Sodium; 2g Fiber.

Yogurt Fruit Dip

A great summertime treat or party dish!

One 8-ounce package cream
    cheese, softened
1 cup nonfat plain yogurt
¼ cup frozen pineapple-orange-
    guava juice concentrate,
    thawed
2 tablespoons honey or rice
    syrup
1 teaspoon fresh lime juice
Fruit for dipping: strawberries,
    cherries, kiwi fruit,
    bananas, etc.

In a medium mixing bowl, combine cream cheese, yogurt, juice concentrate, honey or rice syrup, and lime juice. Beat at medium speed of electric mixer until smooth and creamy. Spoon into serving dish and serve with fruit.

Makes 2 cups

VARIATION

Substitute a fruit-flavored yogurt, such as strawberry, for plain yogurt; omit honey.

Per Tablespoon:
38 Calories; 1g Protein; 3g Fat;
3g Carbohydrates; 8mg Cholesterol; 29mg Sodium; 0 Fiber.

Caribbean Snack Mix

This recipe offers a zesty twist on traditional trail mixes.

SEASONING MIX:

1 tablespoon sugar
1 teaspoon ground cinnamon
**¼ teaspoon freshly ground
    black pepper**
¼ teaspoon ground allspice
⅛ teaspoon cayenne pepper

FRUIT MIX:

**3 cups broken graham crackers
    (broken into bite-size
    pieces)**
1 cup dried banana chips
1 cup peanuts
**One 3-ounce package dried
    mango, chopped (about
    ¾ cup)**
**One 3-ounce package dried
    papaya, chopped (about
    ½ cup)**
½ cup chopped dried pineapple
Nonstick cooking spray

In a small bowl, combine seasoning mix ingredients. Set aside.

In a large bowl, combine fruit mix ingredients. Spray fruit mix lightly with nonstick cooking spray. Toss mix lightly; spray again. Sprinkle fruit mix with half of seasoning mix; toss to coat. Sprinkle with remaining seasoning mix; toss to coat.

Makes 6¼ cups; 12 servings

Per Serving:
197 Calories; 4g Protein; 10g Fat;
25g Carbohydrates; 0 Cholesterol;
87mg Sodium; 3g Fiber.

Artichoke Kebabs

This appetizer couldn't be simpler, and it makes a pretty display on a buffet table.

One 14-ounce can small
  artichoke hearts in water,
  drained and halved
½ medium green bell pepper,
  cut into about nine 1-inch
  squares
½ medium red bell pepper, cut
  into about nine 1-inch
  squares
Six 6-inch wooden skewers
½ cup nonfat Italian dressing
  or other vinaigrette

Thread artichokes and pepper chunks evenly on skewers. Place kebabs in a shallow dish. Pour dressing evenly over kebabs, turning to coat. Serve.

Makes 6 kebabs; 6 servings

VARIATIONS

Add olives, hearts of palm, or chunks of summer squash to skewers in addition to or in place or artichokes and peppers.

Per Serving:
48 Calories; 3g Protein; <1g Fat;
10g Carbohydrates; 0 Cholesterol;
290mg Sodium; 4g Fiber.

Mini Mexican Pita Pizzas

Pizzas made on pita "crusts" make wonderful finger food. Make sure you get the soft pita breads, known as pita folds, as opposed to pita pockets, or your pizzas will be overly crisp.

4 soft pita folds
Nonstick cooking spray
½ teaspoon garlic powder
1 cup peeled and julienned
**   jícama (see Helpful Hint)**
1 cup shredded pepper cheese
½ teaspoon ground cumin
½ cup chunky salsa or to taste
Snipped fresh cilantro

Preheat oven to 400°F.

Arrange pita on large baking sheet. Spray tops of pitas with nonstick cooking spray. Sprinkle evenly with garlic powder. Top pitas evenly with jícama, cheese, and cumin. Bake pizzas until cheese is melted and golden brown, about 15 minutes. Top evenly with salsa and cilantro.

Makes 4 pizzas; 8 servings

VARIATIONS

For a Hawaiian pizza, top the pitas with one 8-ounce can pineapple tidbits or crushed pineapple, drained; ½ cup sliced scallions; 2½ tablespoons sliced and drained pimiento (or finely chopped red bell pepper); and 1 cup shredded smoked gouda cheese.

For an Italian pizza, top with 1 cup coarsely chopped fresh spinach, ½ cup crumbled goat cheese (chèvre), ¼ cup drained and slivered oil-packed sun-dried tomatoes, and ¼ cup pine nuts.

Helpful Hint

Jícama is a tan root vegetable popular in Mexican cuisine. It has a crisp, white flesh with a flavor similar to a pear, but less sweet. Jícama is sold in the produce section of most supermarkets and in Latin American groceries.

Per Serving:
151 Calories; 6g Protein; 5g Fat; 20g Carbohydrates; 12mg Cholesterol; 351mg Sodium; 1g Fiber.

CHAPTER 2

Main Dishes

Caribbean Bean Burgers

One 15-ounce can great northern beans, rinsed and drained
1 cup plain bread crumbs
¼ cup finely chopped onion
1 egg, slightly beaten
3 tablespoons skim milk
1 clove garlic, minced
1 teaspoon Jamaican jerk seasoning (see Helpful Hint)
¼ teaspoon salt
Nonstick cooking spray
4 whole grain hamburger buns or 8 slices whole grain bread

In a medium mixing bowl, mash beans with a fork until smooth. Stir in remaining ingredients (except buns or bread); mix well.

Shape mixture into 4 patties, about 4 inches in diameter. Spray a nonstick skillet with nonstick cooking spray. Heat skillet over medium heat. Cook patties in skillet until browned, turning once, about 8 minutes. Serve burgers on buns or bread with your favorite burger condiments.

Makes 4 burgers; 4 servings

Helpful Hint

Jamaican jerk seasoning is available in the spice section of most grocery stores. It is a dry spice blend that usually includes garlic, chile peppers, thyme, onions, and a variety of other spices.

Per Serving:
332 Calories; 17g Protein; 5g Fat; 53g Carbohydrates; 53mg Cholesterol; 107mg Sodium; 13g Fiber.

Barbados Black Bean Cakes with Mango Salsa

MANGO SALSA:

2 cups peeled, diced mango
½ cup diced red bell pepper
¼ cup finely diced red onion
1 serrano pepper, seeded and minced
2 tablespoons coarsely chopped fresh cilantro
2 teaspoons minced fresh ginger root
1 tablespoon fresh lime juice

BLACK BEAN CAKES:

Two 15-ounce cans black beans, rinsed and drained
¼ cup chopped fresh cilantro
¼ cup finely chopped red onion
1 egg white, slightly beaten
1 teaspoon ground cumin
1 teaspoon minced garlic
½ teaspoon ground allspice
⅛ teaspoon cayenne pepper
⅓ cup dry whole wheat bread crumbs
Nonstick cooking spray
1 tablespoon olive oil
Chopped fresh cilantro and lime wedges for garnish (optional)

Combine all mango salsa ingredients in a bowl. Set aside.

For the black bean cakes, place beans in a large bowl and coarsely mash until they stick together. Add cilantro, onion, egg white, cumin, garlic, allspice, and cayenne pepper. Mix until well blended.

Divide bean mixture into 8 equal parts. Shape into ½-inch-thick patties. Coat patties with bread crumbs. Spray both sides of patties with nonstick cooking spray.

Heat oil in a skillet over medium-high heat. Add bean cakes and fry until golden brown on both sides, turning once, about 8 minutes total. Serve warm with mango salsa. Garnish with cilantro and lime wedges, if desired.

Makes 8 cakes; 4 servings

Per Serving:
424 Calories; 19g Protein; 5g Fat; 75g Carbohydrates; 0 Cholesterol; 81mg Sodium; 13g Fiber.

Mexican Lasagna

1 teaspoon olive oil

1 medium onion, chopped (about 1 cup)

1 medium green bell pepper, coarsely chopped (about 1¼ cups)

1 to 2 cloves garlic, minced

1 to 2 tablespoons chili powder

1 teaspoon ground cumin

Dash cayenne pepper

One 15½-ounce can pinto or kidney beans, rinsed and drained

1 cup frozen or fresh corn kernels

1 cup tomato sauce

Nonstick cooking spray

Six small corn tortillas

1 cup nonfat or low-fat cottage cheese

½ to 1 cup shredded cheddar cheese

Preheat the oven to 375°F.

In a large, nonstick skillet, heat oil over medium-high heat. Add onion, bell pepper, and garlic and cook, stirring, until tender, about 5 minutes. Stir in chili powder, cumin, and cayenne pepper, and cook 1 minute more. Stir in beans, corn, and tomato sauce. Remove from heat.

Spread 3 tortillas over bottom of a 2-quart casserole that has been sprayed with nonstick cooking spray. Spoon half of bean mixture over tortillas. Top with half of cottage cheese. Sprinkle half of cheddar cheese over cottage cheese. Repeat layers.

Bake until casserole is heated through and cheese is melted, about 20 minutes.

Makes 4 to 6 servings

Per Serving:
344 Calories; 20g Protein; 7g Fat; 53g Carbohydrates; 20mg Cholesterol; 759mg Sodium; 9g Fiber.

Quick Bean-and-Rice Burritos

1 cup uncooked basmati or
    quick-cooking brown rice
12 small flour tortillas
One 15½-ounce can black
    beans, undrained
1 clove garlic, minced
1 medium tomato, chopped
¼ cup chopped onion
1 to 2 teaspoons chili powder or
    to taste
½ teaspoon ground cumin or to
    taste
Chopped scallions and salsa for
    garnish

Prepare the rice according to the package directions. Meanwhile, wrap tortillas in aluminum foil and place in a 200°F oven to warm.

Combine beans, bean liquid, garlic, tomato, onion, chili powder, and cumin in a saucepan. Simmer until tomato begins to soften, about 5 minutes.

Remove tortillas from oven. Place a heaping tablespoon of rice and 1 to 2 tablespoons of bean mixture in a warm tortilla. Garnish with scallions and salsa, and roll up tortillas, folding in sides to enclose fillings.

Makes 12 burritos; 6 servings

VARIATIONS

Omit the tortillas, make additional rice, and serve bean mixture over rice.

Add additional toppings, such as grated carrot, shredded lettuce, nonfat plain yogurt, or low-fat sour cream, sliced avocado, chopped bell peppers, shredded cheese, or sliced olives.

Per Serving:
468 Calories; 16g Protein; 8g Fat; 82g Carbohydrates; 0 Cholesterol; 418mg Sodium; 8g Fiber.

Picadillo Tortillas

6 large corn or flour tortillas

PICADILLO:

2 teaspoons canola oil
**1 small onion, finely chopped
    (about ½ cup)**
**One 15½-ounce can red kidney
    beans, rinsed, drained, and
    slightly mashed**
**One 15½-ounce can pinto
    beans, rinsed, drained, and
    slightly mashed**
1 cup chunky picante sauce
¼ cup raisins
1 teaspoon chili powder
½ teaspoon ground cumin
Dash ground cinnamon

SALSA:

1½ cups chunky picante sauce
**1 cup frozen corn kernels,
    thawed**

GARNISH:

1 tomato, seeded and chopped
Sliced black olives

Preheat oven to 350°F. Wrap tortillas in aluminum foil and heat in oven for 15 minutes.

Meanwhile, to make the picadillo, heat oil in a large skillet over medium heat. Add onion and cook, stirring, until tender, about 3 minutes. Stir in remaining picadillo ingredients. Simmer until heated through, stirring frequently, about 5 minutes.

For the salsa, combine picante sauce and corn and set aside.

To serve, spoon ½ cup picadillo across center of each tortilla. Roll up tortillas. Top tortillas evenly with salsa and garnish with tomato and black olives.

Makes 6 tortillas; 6 servings

VARIATIONS

Place 1 strip of green chile on picadillo before rolling up tortilla.

Add additional garnishes of guacamole or low-fat sour cream.

Per Tortilla:
252 Calories; 10g Protein; 3g Fat; 49g Carbohydrates; 0 Cholesterol; 1,027mg Sodium; 10g Fiber.

Black Bean Flautas

Two 15½-ounce cans black
  beans, undrained
2 teaspoons chili powder or to
  taste
½ teaspoon ground cumin
1 clove garlic, minced
1 bay leaf
12 small flour tortillas
6 scallions, minced
2 tomatoes, chopped
1 cup grated cheddar or soy
  cheese
Salsa, sour cream, or yogurt for
  garnish (optional)

In a medium saucepan, combine beans, bean liquid, chili powder, cumin, garlic, and bay leaf. Simmer over medium-low heat for 5 minutes. Remove bay leaf and discard. Drain bean mixture, reserving liquid. Mash beans, adding back liquid as needed for desired consistency. (Bean mixture should resemble a thick puree.)

Preheat oven to 400°F.

Place 1 or 2 heaping table-spoons of bean mixture in the center of each tortilla; spread mixture out a bit with the back of a spoon. Top with some scallions, tomatoes, and cheese. Roll up into a tube shape; place in a 9x13-inch baking pan, seam-side down. Continue until you've used all of the tortillas.

Bake until lightly browned, about 15 minutes. Use leftover bean mixture, salsa, sour cream, or yogurt for garnish.

Makes 12 flautas; 12 servings

VARIATION

For faster preparation but a slightly different flavor, substitute canned refried beans for mashed black beans and spices.

Per Serving:
350 Calories; 16g Protein; 10g Fat; 50g Carbohydrates; 20mg Cholesterol; 350mg Sodium; 6g Fiber.

Bean Quesadillas

One 15½-ounce can black, red, or pinto beans, rinsed and drained

¼ cup chopped tomato

3 tablespoons chopped fresh cilantro

12 large black olives, pitted and sliced

8 small whole wheat or corn tortillas

1 cup (4 ounces) low-fat jalapeño-jack cheese or soy cheese, shredded

10 ounces (1 bag) fresh spinach leaves, stemmed and shredded

¼ cup salsa

Preheat oven to 350°F.

In a large bowl, mash beans with a potato masher or wooden spoon. Stir in tomato, cilantro, and olives. Spread bean mixture evenly over 4 tortillas. Sprinkle evenly with cheese, spinach, and salsa. Top with remaining tortillas.

Place quesadillas on an ungreased baking sheet and bake until cheese melts, about 10 to 12 minutes. Cut into wedges and serve hot.

Makes 4 quesadillas; 4 servings

Per Serving:
406 Calories; 26g Protein; 8g Fat; 71g Carbohydrates; 20mg Cholesterol; 906mg Sodium; 17g Fiber.

Southwestern Vegetable Burritos

*Bottled salsa, canned beans, and packaged shredded cheese will speed
preparation of this traditional Mexican dish.*

**6 large whole wheat or regular
   tortillas**
1 tablespoon canola oil
**1 medium sweet or yellow
   onion, coarsely chopped**
**1 large red bell pepper, coarsely
   chopped**
**1 large green bell pepper,
   coarsely chopped**
2 large cloves garlic, minced
**1 cup salsa, plus more for
   garnish and dipping**
1 teaspoon ground cumin
**One 15½-ounce can pinto
   beans, drained**
1 ripe avocado
½ cup chopped cilantro
**1 cup (4 ounces) shredded
   low-fat cheddar cheese
   (optional)**

Preheat oven to 350°F. Wrap
tortillas in aluminum foil. Bake 15
minutes or until heated through.

Meanwhile, heat oil in a large
nonstick skillet over medium-high
heat. Add onion, bell peppers,
and garlic; cook 3 minutes,
stirring frequently. Add salsa and
cumin. Cover, reduce heat, and
simmer until vegetables are
tender, about 5 minutes.

Meanwhile, place beans in
medium bowl. Partially mash with
potato masher or back of wooden
spoon. Stir beans into vegetable
mixture; cover and cook until
heated through, about 5 minutes.

Peel, pit, and dice avocado;
place in small bowl and set aside.
Remove vegetable mixture from
heat; stir in cilantro.

Spoon about ½ cup vegetable-
bean mixture down center of each
warm tortilla; top with avocado.
Sprinkle with cheese if desired.
Roll and serve immediately with
additional salsa if desired.

Makes 6 burritos; 6 servings

Per Serving:
233 Calories; 7g Protein; 8g Fat; 39g
Carbohydrates; 0 Cholesterol;
730mg Sodium; 10g Fiber.

Brazilian Vegetable Feijoada

In Brazil, a feijoada completa *is a large, festive meal with at least one dish based on beans. This Brazilian Vegetable Feijoada is flavorful yet simple to prepare.*

2 tablespoons olive oil
¼ teaspoon red pepper flakes
1 teaspoon ground cumin
1 teaspoon ground thyme
2 medium sweet potatoes, peeled and chopped
1 large leek (white part only), cut into ½-inch slices
1 red bell pepper, cut length-wise into ½-inch slices
1 yellow bell pepper, cut length-wise into ½-inch slices
1 medium yellow onion, sliced into ½-inch crescents
1 tablespoon dark rum
2 tablespoons fresh lime juice
1 large tomato, cut lengthwise into ½-inch slices
Nonstick cooking spray
Two 15½-ounce cans black beans, drained and rinsed
Chopped fresh cilantro to taste
Cooked rice or other grain (optional)

In a large pot over medium heat, heat oil. Add pepper flakes, cumin, and thyme, and cook, stirring, until fragrant, about 20 seconds. Add sweet potatoes and cook for 5 minutes, stirring occasionally.

Add leek and cook for 5 minutes more, stirring occasionally. Stir in peppers and onion and cook for 5 minutes. Add rum and lime juice. Cook until sweet potatoes are tender, about 5 minutes more. Stir in tomato.

Spray a small saucepan with nonstick cooking spray. Add beans and cook until hot, about 3 minutes. (Add water a little at a time to prevent sticking.) To serve, pour beans in a casserole, serving bowl, or platter, and pour sweet potato mixture on top of beans. Garnish with cilantro.

If serving over rice or other grain, form a ring around serving platter with rice or grain, pour beans into center of platter, and top with sweet potato mixture. Garnish with cilantro.

Makes 6 servings

Per Serving:
305 Calories; 10g Protein; 5g Fat; 54g Carbohydrates; 0 Cholesterol; 22mg Sodium; 12g Fiber.

Tandoori-Style Chickpeas

2 teaspoons canola oil
1 cup chopped onion
1 cup chopped green bell pepper
½ cup chopped red bell pepper
3 cloves garlic, minced
1 teaspoon minced fresh ginger root
1 tablespoon curry powder
One 15½-ounce can low-sodium or regular stewed tomatoes
One 15½-ounce can chickpeas (garbanzo beans), rinsed and drained
¾ cup water or tomato juice
½ of a 10-ounce package frozen spinach, thawed
2 cups chopped cauliflower
¼ teaspoon salt
¼ teaspoon cayenne pepper or to taste

Heat oil in a large nonstick skillet over moderate heat. Add onion, peppers, garlic, and ginger; cook, stirring, until fragrant, about 2 minutes. Add curry powder; cook 3 minutes, stirring. Add tomatoes and chickpeas; bring to a boil, stirring. Slowly add water or tomato juice, and spinach, stirring constantly.

Place cauliflower on top of stew. Cover; simmer until cauliflower is tender, about 10 minutes. Season with salt and cayenne pepper.

Makes 6 servings

Per Serving:
160 Calories; 7g Protein; 3g Fat; 30g Carbohydrates; 0 Cholesterol; 543mg Sodium; 8g Fiber.

Dirty Rice with Beans

Dirty rice is a traditional Cajun dish that gets its name from the "dirty" look of the rice from the meat used in the dish. Here's a dirty rice that's meatless.

1 cup quick-cooking brown rice
One 8-ounce package frozen vegetarian "sausage" patties, thawed, cut into chunks
½ cup sliced celery
½ cup chopped red bell pepper
½ cup chopped onion
1 clove garlic, minced
One 15½-ounce can butter beans, rinsed and drained
½ teaspoon freshly ground black pepper
¼ to ½ teaspoon cayenne pepper
¼ teaspoon ground cumin
¼ teaspoon dried thyme leaves
¼ teaspoon salt

Prepare rice according to package directions. Fluff with a fork.

Meanwhile, spray a large nonstick skillet with vegetable cooking spray. Heat skillet over medium heat. Add "sausage," celery, bell pepper, onion, and garlic. Cook, stirring, until vegetables are tender-crisp and "sausage" is browned, about 5 minutes.

Add cooked rice and all remaining ingredients to skillet; mix well. Reduce heat to medium-low. Cook until heated through, about 3 minutes, stirring occasionally.

Makes 4 servings

Per Serving:
371 Calories; 15g Protein; 3g Fat; 70g Carbohydrates; 1mg Cholesterol; 650mg Sodium; 12g Fiber.

Grilled Mediterranean Vegetables with Couscous

2 baby eggplants or Japanese eggplants (about 8 ounces), ends trimmed, and halved lengthwise

2 small zucchini (about 8 ounces), ends trimmed and halved lengthwise

2 small yellow summer squash (about 8 ounces), ends trimmed and halved lengthwise

1 large red bell pepper, quartered

1 large yellow bell pepper, quartered

2 to 3 tablespoons garlic-infused olive oil (see Helpful Hint)

One 14½-ounce can vegetable broth (about 2 cups)

1 cup whole wheat or regular couscous

Salt and freshly ground black pepper to taste

1 tablespoon porcini-, basil- or rosemary-infused olive oil (optional; see Helpful Hint)

Preheat grill. Brush both sides of eggplants, squash, and bell peppers with garlic oil. Arrange vegetables on grill rack over medium-hot coals. Grill until tender, turning once, 10 to 12 minutes.

Meanwhile, bring broth to a boil in a medium saucepan. Stir in couscous; remove from heat. Cover; let stand until liquid is absorbed, about 5 minutes. Spoon onto 4 warmed serving plates; top with grilled vegetables. Season with salt and pepper to taste. Drizzle with flavored oil, if desired.

Makes 4 servings

Helpful Hint

Infused and flavored oils are available in gourmet markets and in some supermarkets. If garlic-infused oil is unavailable, substitute 3 tablespoons olive oil combined with 2 cloves minced garlic.

Per Serving:
305 Calories; 8g Protein; 7g Fat; 57g Carbohydrates; 0 Cholesterol; 129mg Sodium; 8g Fiber.

Six-Vegetable Couscous

COUSCOUS:

1½ cups whole wheat or
   regular couscous
3 cups boiling water
1 tablespoon butter or canola
   oil
1 teaspoon turmeric
1 teaspoon salt

VEGETABLES:

2 tablespoons canola oil
2 medium onions, chopped
1 cup finely shredded cabbage
1 medium turnip, peeled and
   diced
1 medium yellow summer
   squash, halved lengthwise
   and cut into ¼-inch slices
1½ cups cooked garbanzo
   beans (chickpeas)
1½ cups diced ripe tomatoes
1 teaspoon grated fresh ginger
   root
½ teaspoon ground cumin
½ teaspoon ground coriander
½ teaspoon turmeric
½ teaspoon salt
Water as needed
Raisins, chopped dried apricots,
   or slivered almonds as
   garnish (optional)

Combine couscous and water in a medium mixing bowl. Cover and let stand until water is absorbed, about 15 minutes. Fluff with a fork. Stir in butter or oil, turmeric, and salt. Cover and set aside.

Meanwhile, heat oil in a large saucepan or soup pot. Add onions and cook, stirring, until tender-crisp, about 3 minutes.

Add all remaining ingredients except water and optional garnishes. Cover and reduce heat to low. Cook, stirring occasionally, for 15 to 20 minutes. Add water as needed to produce a moist, but not soupy, stew.

Arrange couscous around outer edge of a large serving platter. Pour vegetable mixture into the center. Garnish stew with raisins, chopped dried apricots, or slivered almonds, if desired.

Makes 8 servings

Per Serving:
265 Calories; 9g Protein; 6g Fat; 46g Carbohydrates; 4mg Cholesterol; 39mg Sodium; 5g Fiber.

Polenta with Three-Mushroom Sauce

*Ready-made polenta is available in most supermarkets these days;
try it for an even faster meal.*

One 14½-ounce can vegetable
  broth (about 2 cups)
1¾ cups water
1 cup coarse yellow cornmeal
2 tablespoons olive oil
½ cup minced shallots or onion
2 cloves garlic, minced
One 3½-ounce package shiitake
  mushroom caps, thinly
  sliced (stems discarded)
One 3½-ounce package oyster
  mushrooms, sliced
4 ounces crimini or button
  mushrooms, sliced
2 large ripe tomatoes, seeded
  and coarsely chopped
1 tablespoon chopped fresh
  thyme leaves or 1 teaspoon
  dried thyme leaves
Salt and freshly ground black
  pepper to taste
Freshly grated Parmesan
  cheese (optional)

In a 3-quart microwave-safe bowl or casserole, whisk together broth, water, and cornmeal. Cover loosely with waxed paper; cook in microwave oven on high power for 6 minutes. Whisk carefully (mixture will be hot); cover and cook until polenta is very thick, 4 to 5 minutes more. Whisk again; cover and let stand until ready to serve.

Heat oil in a large nonstick skillet over medium heat. Add shallots or onion, and garlic; cook, stirring, 1 minute. Add mushrooms; cook until mushrooms are tender, about 5 minutes.

Add tomatoes and thyme to mushroom mixture. Cook until heated through, stirring occasionally, 3 to 4 minutes. Season to taste with salt and pepper. Spoon polenta onto 4 warm serving plates; top with mushroom mixture and cheese if desired.

Makes 4 servings

Per Serving:
308 Calories; 8g Protein;
56g Carbohydrates; 0 Cholesterol;
181mg Sodium; 7g Fiber.

Asian Noodle Salad

One 5-ounce package uncooked
  Japanese curly noodles (see
  Helpful Hints), broken into
  thirds

DRESSING:

3 tablespoons soy sauce
3 tablespoons rice vinegar (see
  Helpful Hints)
2 teaspoons garlic-flavored oil
  (see Helpful Hints) or
  sesame oil
½ teaspoon sugar
½ teaspoon five-spice powder
  (see Helpful Hints)

SALAD:

1 cup snow pea pods, trimmed
1 cup shredded red cabbage
1 cup julienned carrots
½ cup sliced celery
½ cup mung bean sprouts
¼ cup sliced scallions
2 teaspoons sesame seeds

Prepare the noodles according to
the package directions; rinse with
cold water and drain.

Meanwhile, combine all dressing ingredients in a 1-cup measure
or small bowl; mix well and set
aside.

In a large bowl, combine
cooked noodles and all salad
ingredients except sesame seeds.
Toss to combine.

Pour dressing over salad; toss
to coat. Sprinkle salad with
sesame seeds.

Makes 4 to 6 servings

Another time-saver

*Buy packaged shredded cabbage
and carrots from the produce
section of your supermarket instead
of shredding them yourself.*

Per Serving:
206 Calories; 10g Protein; 3g Fat;
38g Carbohydrates; 0 Cholesterol;
815mg Sodium; 7g Fiber.

Helpful Hints

Japanese curly noodles, also called chuka soba, *are available in the soup or noodle aisle of most supermarkets. Ramen noodles can be substituted (save the seasoning packet for another use); however, many ramen noodles are fried and are high in fat. Be sure to buy the baked variety.*

Garlic-flavored oil and other flavored and infused oils are available in many supermarkets, natural foods stores, and gourmet shops.

Rice vinegar is a mild vinegar made from rice that is a popular seasoning in Asian cuisines. It is excellent in sauces and salads. Rice vinegar is available in Asian markets, natural food stores, and in most supermarkets.

Chinese five-spice powder is a mixture of equal parts of cinnamon, cloves, fennel seed, star anise, and Szechuan peppercorns. It is sold in some supermarkets and in Chinese groceries, and is easily made at home.

Spicy Spanish Rice

Smoked gouda cheese gives this colorful dish a rich and hearty flavor and texture. It's ready in twenty-five minutes.

2 teaspoons canola oil
1 cup chopped green bell
    pepper
½ cup chopped onion
1 to 2 cloves garlic, minced
1½ cups quick-cooking brown
    rice
One 14½-ounce can diced
    tomatoes with green chile
    peppers
1 cup water
1½ teaspoons chili powder
⅛ teaspoon black pepper
One 15½-ounce can red kidney
    beans, rinsed and drained
¼ to ½ cup (about 2 ounces)
    shredded smoked gouda
    cheese

Heat the oil in a medium nonstick skillet over medium heat. Add the bell pepper, onion, and garlic; cook, stirring, until onion is tender, about 5 minutes. Add the rice, tomatoes, water, chili powder, and black pepper. Bring to a boil over high heat. Reduce heat to medium-low. Cover and simmer for 5 minutes.

Add the beans and cheese. Cook until rice is done and cheese is melted, stirring frequently.

Makes 3 to 4 servings

VARIATION

For a milder tasting dish, substitute plain canned diced tomatoes for tomatoes with chile peppers.

Per Serving:
384 Calories; 16g Protein; 7g Fat; 63g Carbohydrates; 11mg Cholesterol; 646mg Sodium; 11g Fiber.

Pasta with Fennel and Walnuts

Toasted walnuts offer a rich, unexpected crunch to this pasta dish.
Fennel bulb gives it a distinct, yet mild flavor.

3 tablespoons chopped walnuts
8 ounces uncooked spaghetti or linguine
1 to 2 tablespoons garlic-flavored oil (see Helpful Hint, p. 39)
1 medium fennel bulb, trimmed (about 6 ounces), cut into thin wedges
2 fresh tomatoes, seeded and coarsely chopped (about 3 cups)
¼ cup coarsely chopped black olives or kalamata olives
¼ teaspoon salt
Freshly ground black pepper to taste
Freshly grated Parmesan cheese (optional)

Preheat oven to 350°F.

Place walnuts in an 8-inch square baking pan. Bake walnuts until toasted and aromatic, shaking pan occasionally, about 10 minutes; set aside.

While walnuts are toasting, cook spaghetti or linguine according to package directions. Drain and keep warm.

Heat oil in a medium nonstick skillet over medium heat. Add the fennel. Cook, stirring, until tender, about 5 minutes.

Stir in tomatoes, olives, salt, and pepper. Cook until hot, about 2 minutes, stirring gently. Add spaghetti or linguine and nuts. Toss to combine. Top with a sprinkling of Parmesan cheese, if desired.

Makes 4 servings

Per Serving:
242 Calories; 7g Protein; 8g Fat; 43g Carbohydrates; 0 Cholesterol; 218mg Sodium; 3g Fiber.

Pasta with Avocado Pesto

**12 ounces uncooked pasta of
your choice (angel hair
works well)**

**2 large or 3 small avocados,
peeled and pitted**

**3 cloves garlic or to taste,
chopped**

**3 tablespoons fresh lemon juice
(juice of 1 lemon)**

**2½ ounces fresh cilantro (about
1 cup packed)**

**⅓ cup freshly grated Parmesan
cheese or to taste**

Prepare the pasta according to
package directions until *al dente*.
Meanwhile, prepare pesto by
combining avocados, garlic, lemon
juice, and cilantro in a food
processor. Process until smooth,
about 1 minute.

Drain pasta and transfer to a
large serving bowl. Pour pesto
over pasta; toss well. Sprinkle
with Parmesan before serving.

Makes 8 servings

Per Serving:
152 Calories; 5g Protein; 8g Fat,
16g Carbohydrates; 0.7mg Cholesterol; 36mg Sodium; 3g Fiber.

Spicy Southwestern Pasta

Italy meets the Southwest in this unusual pairing,
and the result is delicious.

1 pound uncooked ziti, fusilli,
    penne, or other short pasta
2 tablespoons olive oil
2½ cups sliced onions
6 cloves garlic, minced
1 yellow bell pepper, cut into
    thin strips
1 pound tomatoes, cubed
Salt and freshly ground black
    pepper to taste
½ cup sliced black or green
    olives
2 to 3 tablespoons capers,
    drained
½ to 1 teaspoon Mexican or
    regular oregano
2 teaspoons red pepper flakes
¼ cup chopped fresh basil
¼ cup chopped fresh cilantro
½ cup freshly grated Monterey
    Jack or Parmesan cheese

Prepare the pasta according to package directions.

Meanwhile, in a large skillet, heat oil over high heat. Add onions, garlic, and bell pepper; cook, stirring, until tender but not brown, about 3 minutes. Add tomatoes, salt, and pepper; cook over high heat until some of the liquid from tomatoes has evaporated, about 5 minutes. Stir in olives, capers, oregano, red pepper flakes, basil, and cilantro. Remove from heat.

Drain pasta into a large bowl. Add tomato mixture; toss together. Sprinkle with cheese and serve.

Makes 6 servings

Per Serving:
379 Calories; 13g Protein; 10g Fat; 62g Carb; 5mg Cholesterol; 615mg Sodium; 5g Fiber.

Fresh Noodles Lo Mein

A fast and favorite recipe of the Vegetarian Times *staff.*

1 tablespoon dark or toasted
    sesame oil (see Helpful
    Hint)
8 ounces firm tofu, drained and
    cut into 1-inch cubes
4 cups vegetable broth
1 tablespoon grated fresh
    ginger root
$\frac{1}{8}$ teaspoon red pepper flakes
    (optional)
3 tablespoons teriyaki sauce
1 large clove garlic, minced
8 ounces fresh linguine
One 1-pound bag frozen
    Oriental-style vegetables
1 small onion, sliced lengthwise
2 scallions, finely sliced

Heat sesame oil in a skillet over medium-high heat, add tofu and sauté until golden brown, about 2 to 3 minutes.

In a large pot, bring vegetable broth to a boil. Add ginger, red pepper flakes if desired, teriyaki sauce, garlic, and linguine. Reduce heat and simmer 2 minutes.

Stir in browned tofu, frozen vegetables, and onion; increase heat and return to a boil. Then reduce heat and simmer 2 minutes more. Stir in scallions. Serve immediately.

Makes 6 servings

Helpful Hint

Dark or toasted sesame oil is more flavorful than the lighter or regular variety. Sesame oil is available in supermarkets, natural food stores, gourmet shops, and Asian markets.

Per Serving:
230 Calories; 12g Protein; 6g Fat; 30g Carbohydrates; 62mg Cholesterol; 432mg Sodium; 4g Fiber.

44

Farfalle with Carrot, Sage, and Scallions

This recipe won first place in the first Vegetarian Times *recipe contest.*

**8 ounces uncooked farfalle
    (bow tie pasta)**
1 teaspoon olive oil
**2 to 3 tablespoons unsalted
    butter**
3 medium carrots, julienned
**9 scallions, cut diagonally into
    1½-inch pieces**
**40 fresh sage leaves, stems
    removed**
**Salt and freshly ground black
    pepper to taste**
Juice of ½ lemon
**3 tablespoons freshly grated
    cheese, such as Monterey
    Jack, Asiago, or Parmesan
    (optional)**

Prepare the farfalle according to package instructions.

Meanwhile, heat a large skillet over medium heat. Add oil and 1½ tablespoons butter. When oil and butter are hot and sizzling, add carrots; cook, stirring, until soft and golden brown, about 7 minutes. Add scallions and sage; cook, stirring, until sage begins to crisp and scallions begin to brown, about 7 minutes. Add salt and pepper to taste. Reduce heat and cover to keep warm.

Drain farfalle and return to cooking pot. Add lemon juice and remaining ½ to 1½ tablespoons butter, or to taste. Toss lightly. Divide farfalle evenly among 3 serving dishes. Top each with carrot-sage mixture. Sprinkle with cheese if desired.

Makes 3 servings

Helpful Hint

Recipe can easily be doubled to serve six.

Per Serving:
329 Calories; 7g Protein; 9g Fat; 53g Carbohydrates; 20mg Cholesterol; 205mg Sodium; 4g Fiber.

Cavatelli with Garden Vegetables and Herbs

12 ounces uncooked cavatelli or orecchiette pasta

2 tablespoons olive oil

6 ounces (about 10) fresh asparagus spears, diagonally sliced into 1-inch pieces

1 red bell pepper, sliced into thin strips

2 to 4 cloves garlic, minced

1 medium yellow squash, halved lengthwise and cut into ½-inch pieces

6 ounces (about 2 cups) sugar snap peas or snow pea pods

One 14½-ounce can vegetable broth (about 2 cups)

⅓ cup snipped or chopped assorted fresh herbs, such as tarragon, thyme, dill, and basil

Salt and freshly ground black pepper to taste

Freshly grated Asiago cheese (optional)

Prepare the cavatelli or orecchiette according to the package directions.

Meanwhile, heat oil in a large saucepan over medium heat. Add asparagus, bell pepper, garlic, squash, peas, and broth to saucepan; bring to a boil over high heat. Reduce heat; simmer uncovered, stirring occasionally, until vegetables are tender-crisp, about 4 to 5 minutes.

Drain cavatelli or orecchiette and transfer to saucepan with the vegetables. Add herbs; toss well. Season with salt and pepper to taste. Serve in shallow soup bowls; sprinkle with cheese if desired.

Makes 6 servings

Per Serving:
297 Calories; 10g Protein; 6g Fat; 52g Carbohydrates; 0 Cholesterol; 209mg Sodium; 5g Fiber.

Mex-Veg Pasta

1 pound uncooked fettuccine or
    linguine
1 tablespoon olive oil
2 cups chopped onion
2 cups chopped green bell
    pepper
½ cup minced mild green chile
    pepper, such as Anaheim or
    poblano
2 cloves garlic, minced
1 teaspoon chili powder
1½ teaspoons dried oregano
2 cups chopped tomatoes
1 cup rinsed and drained
    canned black beans
Corn kernels sliced from 1 ear
    (about ½ cup kernels)
1 tablespoon finely chopped
    fresh cilantro
Juice of 1 lime
Salt to taste

Prepare the fettuccine or linguine according to package directions; drain. Rinse under cold water; set aside.

Meanwhile, heat oil in a nonstick skillet over medium heat. Add onion and peppers; cook, stirring frequently, 2 to 3 minutes. Add garlic, chili powder, oregano, tomatoes, beans, and corn; cook, stirring, 2 to 3 minutes more. Add cooked fettuccine or linguine and cilantro; sauté until pasta and vegetables are heated through, about 1 minute. Sprinkle lime juice over pasta; add salt.

Makes 6 servings

Per Serving:
357 Calories; 12g Protein; 4g Fat;
70g Carbohydrates; 0 Cholesterol;
117mg Sodium; 8g Fiber.

Tuscan Penne with Cannellini Beans and Garlic

8 ounces uncooked penne
1 tablespoon olive oil
2 cloves garlic, minced
1 teaspoon dried oregano
1 cup chopped red onion
1 cup diced red bell pepper
1 cup diced fennel bulb
1 cup diced zucchini
1 cup diced tomato
One 15½-ounce can cannellini beans, rinsed and drained
4 cups chopped escarole (see Helpful Hints)
1 cup vegetable broth or roasted garlic broth (see Helpful Hints)
1 teaspoon salt
Freshly ground black pepper to taste

Prepare the penne according to package directions. Drain and rinse with cold water; set aside.

Heat oil in a large nonstick sauté pan over medium-high heat. Add garlic, oregano, onion, bell pepper, fennel, and zucchini; cook, stirring, 2 minutes. Add tomato; cook 1 minute more. Add beans, cooked penne pasta, escarole, and broth. Simmer until vegetables are tender and escarole wilts, about 3 minutes. Add salt and pepper.

Makes 6 servings

Helpful Hints

Escarole, a member of the endive family, is a leafy green with a mildly bitter flavor.

To make roasted garlic broth: Preheat oven to 375°F. Slice 2 whole garlic bulbs in half crosswise. Sprinkle cut surfaces lightly with olive oil, and salt and pepper if desired. Wrap tightly in foil; bake until tender, about 40 minutes.

In a soup pot, add 2 quarts water, any accumulated vegetable trimmings and roasted garlic. Simmer 45 minutes, adding herbs such as thyme, rosemary, oregano, or basil to taste. Strain broth; cool. Broth can be kept up to 1 week in the refrigerator. Or freeze broth in ice cube trays, and pack frozen broth cubes in resealable plastic bags to store in freezer.

Per Serving:
318 Calories; 13g Protein; 3g Fat; 59g Carbohydrates; 0 Cholesterol; 1,077mg Sodium; 8g Fiber

Vermicelli Florentine

1 large onion
1 teaspoon canola oil
¼ cup water
½ cup buttermilk
2 teaspoons cornstarch
1 to 2 teaspoons soy sauce or ¼ teaspoon salt
2½ ounces whole wheat vermicelli or linguine
3 medium tomatoes, blanched and seeded, and cut into 1-inch chunks (see Helpful Hint)
⅔ cup small or regular peas, fresh or frozen and thawed
1 to 2 bunches spinach (about 12 ounces), washed, stemmed and cut into ¾-inch strips
Freshly grated Parmesan cheese (optional)

Slice onion paper thin. In a large, heavy skillet, cook the onion in oil and water. Keep heat low and stir frequently until onion is golden brown. Remove onion from skillet.

In a small bowl, stir together buttermilk, cornstarch, and soy sauce or salt. Pour into a skillet. Bring to a boil, stirring constantly. Mixture will curdle but will then come together in a smooth sauce.

Cook vermicelli or linguine according to package directions. While pasta is cooking, add onions, tomatoes, and peas to buttermilk mixture, and heat. Gently stir spinach into sauce. When pasta is done, drain and stir into sauce. Add Parmesan cheese if desired. Serve immediately.

Makes 2 servings

Helpful Hint

To blanch tomatoes, place in boiling water for a minute, then plunge into cold water; slip off skins.

Per Serving:
300 Calories; 15g Protein; 4g Fat; 48g Carbohydrates; 60mg Cholesterol; 44mg Sodium; 13g Fiber.

Thai Noodles

Pasta doesn't just mean Italian.
Here, linguine is transformed into an Asian dish.

1 pound uncooked or fresh linguine
2 tablespoons peanut oil
2 cloves garlic, minced
3 scallions, sliced diagonally into ½-inch slices
¼ cup soy sauce
3 tablespoons fresh lime juice
1 teaspoon sugar
¼ teaspoon red pepper flakes
½ to ¾ cup chopped, unsalted peanuts
2 cups mung bean sprouts

Prepare linguine according to package directions until *al dente*; drain. Transfer to a large serving bowl; set aside.

Meanwhile, in a medium skillet, heat oil over medium heat. Add garlic and scallions and cook, stirring, for 2 minutes. Add soy sauce, lime juice, and sugar. Cook for 1 minute more.

Pour soy sauce mixture over linguine. Add remaining ingredients and toss to combine.

Makes 6 to 8 servings

Per Serving:
219 Calories; 8g Protein; 10g Fat; 23g Carbohydrates; 0 Cholesterol; 598mg Sodium; 3g Fiber.

Pesto Primavera

2 cups broccoli florets
½ medium red bell pepper, julienned
1 cup sliced button mushrooms
½ cup julienned carrots
1 cup sliced zucchini
2 tablespoons water
8 ounces uncooked fettuccine
1 cup fresh basil
¼ cup nonfat Italian salad dressing
1 to 2 cloves garlic, halved
2 tablespoons olive oil
1 tablespoon freshly grated Parmesan cheese
¼ teaspoon grated lemon peel

In a 2-quart casserole, combine broccoli, bell pepper, mushrooms, carrots, zucchini, and water; microwave until tender, 6 to 8 minutes, stirring once. Drain and set aside.

Prepare the fettuccine according to package directions; drain and set aside.

While fettuccine is cooking, place basil, salad dressing, garlic, oil, cheese, and lemon peel in a food processor or blender and process until smooth.

To serve, place fettuccine on plates or serving platter, add pesto, toss to combine, and top with vegetables.

Makes 4 servings

Per Serving:
310 Calories; 10g Protein; 7g Fat; 50g Carbohydrates; 1mg Cholesterol; 84mg Sodium; 5g Fiber.

Creamy Light Fettuccine Alfredo

12 ounces uncooked fettuccine, preferably whole wheat
2 cups evaporated skim milk or low-fat soy milk (see Helpful Hint)
4 cloves garlic, minced or pressed
6 tablespoons freshly grated Parmesan cheese
¼ cup chopped fresh parsley
Freshly ground black pepper to taste
2 cups chopped and steamed vegetables of your choice: carrots, green beans, zucchini, onions, broccoli, or peas

Prepare the fettuccine according to package directions; drain. Transfer pasta to a large nonstick sauté pan; add milk and garlic. Bring to a simmer, stirring frequently. Add cheese.

Continue cooking until cheese melts and sauce thickens. Stir in parsley and black pepper. Add steamed vegetables, toss gently, and serve immediately.

Makes 4 servings

VARIATIONS

Add 1 teaspoon curry powder with the fettuccine, milk, and garlic.

Helpful Hint

You may substitute 1½ cups powdered skim milk mixed with 1½ cups water for the evaporated milk.

Per Serving:
416 Calories; 25g Protein; 4g Fat; 68g Carbohydrates; 150mg Cholesterol; 343mg Sodium; 4g Fiber.

Pasta and Navy Beans in Tomato Sauce

12 ounces uncooked penne or rotini pasta

½ cup water

1 teaspoon olive oil

3 cloves garlic (or to taste), slivered

3 plum tomatoes or 1 large regular tomato, chopped

2 cups low-sodium or regular tomato sauce

3 sprigs fresh parsley, chopped

2 teaspoons dried oregano

2 teaspoons dried basil

2 cups broccoli florets

2 cups cooked or canned navy beans, drained

¼ cup slivered black olives

Salt and freshly ground black pepper to taste

Chopped fresh parsley for garnish

Cook penne or rotini pasta according to package directions. Drain well.

Meanwhile, in a large pot, combine ¼ cup water with olive oil, and bring to a boil; add garlic and cook, stirring, until lightly browned. Stir in remaining ¼ cup water, tomatoes, tomato sauce, parsley, oregano, and basil. Cook, uncovered, over medium heat, mashing tomatoes with a spoon, until sauce thickens, about 8 minutes. Add broccoli. Simmer, covered, until broccoli is tender but still crunchy, about 5 more minutes.

Add beans and olives, and mix well. Simmer, covered, until heated through. Stir in pasta. Add salt and pepper to taste, sprinkle with parsley, and serve immediately.

Makes 5 servings

Per Serving:
432 Calories; 18g Protein; 5g Fat; 77g Carbohydrates; 0 Cholesterol; 144mg Sodium; 18g Fiber.

Mostaccioli Primavera

Enjoy fresh farmers' market produce in this light and flavorful dish.
Substitute other vegetables for those in this recipe to create your own
colorful combo.

2 cups uncooked mostaccioli
3 teaspoons olive oil, divided
4 cloves garlic, minced
One 14-ounce can diced low-
**   sodium or regular toma-**
**   toes, undrained**
One 8-ounce can low-sodium or
**   regular tomato sauce**
½ teaspoon dried rosemary,
**   crushed**
¼ teaspoon fennel seeds,
**   crushed**
½ red bell pepper, cut into
**   strips**
½ green bell pepper, cut into
**   strips**
½ cup sliced zucchini (cut in
**   half lengthwise and sliced)**
½ cup sliced yellow summer
**   squash (cut in half length-**
**   wise and sliced)**
1 small onion, cut into 6
**   wedges and separated**

Prepare mostaccioli according to
package directions.

Meanwhile, heat 2 teaspoons
oil in a 2-quart saucepan over
medium heat. Add garlic. Cook for
1 minute, stirring constantly. Add
tomatoes, tomato sauce, rosemary,
and fennel seeds. Bring to a
simmer and reduce heat to low.
Simmer for 15 minutes to blend
flavors. Set sauce aside.

In a medium nonstick skillet,
heat remaining 1 teaspoon oil over
medium heat. Add peppers, zucchini, yellow squash, and onion.
Cook, stirring, just until onion is
tender-crisp, about 5 minutes.

Drain mostaccioli. In a large
serving bowl, combine pasta,
sauce, and vegetables. Toss to
coat. Serve immediately.

Makes 4 to 6 servings

Per Serving:
334 Calories; 12g Protein; 4g Fat;
64g Carbohydrates; 0 Cholesterol;
381mg Sodium; 5g Fiber.

Pad Thai

**8 to 10 ounces flat rice noodles,
    uncooked**
¼ cup white vinegar
3 tablespoons tomato paste
3 tablespoons water
2 tablespoons sugar
1 to 2 tablespoons canola oil
2 cloves garlic, minced
**1 fresh green chile pepper,
    seeded and minced**
2 eggs
1 cup fresh mung bean sprouts
**⅓ cup chopped unsalted, dry-
    roasted peanuts**
**Lime wedges and sliced
    scallions**

Bring 2 quarts water to a boil and remove from heat. Soak noodles in water for 20 minutes. Drain and set aside.

While noodles soak, mix together vinegar, tomato paste, water, and sugar in a bowl. Set aside.

In a large skillet, heat oil and stir-fry garlic and chile pepper over medium heat for 3 minutes. Stir in tomato-vinegar mixture and make a well in center of pan. Crack eggs into well, and cook until almost set, about 2 minutes, then stir quickly into sauce.

Let sauce continue to simmer on low heat until very thick, about 4 to 5 minutes. Toss noodles into sauce and mix well. Remove from heat.

To serve, place noodles and sauce on one end of a serving platter. On the other end, place mounds of bean sprouts and peanuts. Garnish with lime wedges and scallions.

Makes 4 servings

VARIATION

Substitute fresh fettuccine for rice noodles, and prepare it according to package directions.

Per Serving:
221 Calories; 9g Protein; 8g Fat; 27g Carbohydrates; 83g Cholesterol; 128mg Sodium; 3g Fiber.

Warm Rotini Salad with Balsamic Vinaigrette

8 ounces uncooked rotini

VINAIGRETTE:

⅓ cup chopped fresh basil
3 tablespoons balsamic vinegar
2 tablespoons olive oil
1 teaspoon brown sugar
½ teaspoon salt

SALAD:

Nonstick cooking spray
2 cups sliced fresh mushrooms
1 medium yellow bell pepper,
seeded and cut into strips
3 cloves garlic, minced
1½ cups halved cherry toma-
toes
¼ cup (1 ounce) cubed fresh
part-skim mozzarella
cheese (optional)
Salt and freshly ground black
pepper to taste

Prepare the rotini according to package directions.

Meanwhile, in a small bowl, combine vinaigrette ingredients. Whisk until well blended. Set aside.

For the salad, spray a medium nonstick skillet with nonstick cooking spray. Cook the mushrooms, bell pepper, and garlic, stirring, over medium heat until tender, about 5 minutes. Add the tomatoes. Cook, stirring constantly, until heated through.

Drain the rotini. In a large bowl, combine rotini and vegetable mixture. Add vinaigrette and cheese, if desired; toss to coat. Season to taste with salt and pepper.

Makes 6 servings

Per Serving:
232 Calories; 8g Protein; 6g Fat; 38g Carbohydrates; 3mg Cholesterol; 207mg Sodium; 2g Fiber.

Ziti with Fresh Tomato-Olive Sauce

*This flavorful dish is much like a main-dish pasta salad,
and is especially good when tomatoes and basil are in season.
It's on the table in twenty-five minutes.*

**8 ounces uncooked ziti or
mostaccioli**
**½ cup pitted and sliced
kalamata olives or one
4-ounce can sliced and
pitted black olives, drained**
⅓ cup thinly sliced fresh basil
1 to 2 tablespoons olive oil
2 tablespoons balsamic vinegar
2 to 4 cloves garlic, minced
**1 tablespoon capers, drained
(optional)**
**½ teaspoon crushed red pepper
flakes**
**1¾ pounds (about 4 large)
tomatoes, coarsely chopped**
**Crumbled goat cheese or
freshly grated Parmesan
cheese to taste (optional)**
**Salt and freshly ground black
pepper to taste**

Prepare the ziti or mostaccioli
according to package directions.

Meanwhile, in a large serving
bowl, combine the olives, basil,
oil, vinegar, garlic, capers if
desired, and red pepper flakes.
Add the tomatoes to the olive
mixture and toss well.

Drain the pasta and add to
tomato-olive sauce; toss well.
Sprinkle with cheese if desired.
Season to taste with salt and
pepper.

Makes about 4 servings

Per Serving:
233 Calories; 5g Protein; 9g Fat;
32g Carbohydrates; 0 Cholesterol;
226mg Sodium; 4g Fiber.

Chinese Vegetables in Peanut Sauce

⅓ cup chunky natural peanut
  butter
3 tablespoons soy sauce or
  tamari (see Helpful Hints)
1 tablespoon brown sugar
One 8-ounce package uncooked
  Chinese noodles (see
  Helpful Hints) or angel-hair
  pasta
¾ cup water or vegetable broth
2 medium carrots, cut into
  matchsticks (about 1 cup)
2 to 3 cloves garlic, minced
1¼ cups sliced fresh shiitake
  mushrooms (3½ ounces)
1 cup snow pea pods, cut
  diagonally into 1-inch
  pieces
½ cup sliced scallions
¼ to ½ teaspoon crushed red
  pepper flakes

In a 1-cup measure or small bowl, combine peanut butter, soy sauce or tamari, and brown sugar; set aside.

Prepare the noodles according to package directions. Drain and rinse with hot water.

Meanwhile, in a medium nonstick skillet, heat water or broth over medium-high heat. Add carrots and garlic; cook, stirring, for 2 minutes. Add mushrooms, pea pods, scallions, and red pepper flakes. Sauté until tender-crisp, about 2 minutes.

Stir in peanut sauce. Cook until smooth and bubbly, about 2 minutes. Pour over hot noodles.

Makes 4 servings

Helpful Hints

Tamari is a variety of Japanese soy sauce that is dark and rich tasting, and usually wheat-free. It is available in supermarkets and natural food stores.

Chinese noodles (also called "plain" Chinese noodles) are very thin, whole wheat noodles sold in the Chinese food section of supermarkets and in Chinese groceries.

Per Serving:
439 Calories; 11g Protein; 10g Fat;
82g Carbohydrates; 0 Cholesterol;
738mg Sodium; 7g Fiber.

Italian Stuffed Shells

12 uncooked jumbo pasta shells
2 teaspoons olive oil
¼ cup chopped onion
2 cloves garlic, minced
1 cup sliced fresh mushrooms
**1 cup sliced yellow summer
    squash**
⅓ cup sliced black olives
**½ teaspoon dried Italian
    seasoning**
**One 26-ounce jar chunky pasta
    sauce**
**Freshly grated Parmesan
    cheese (optional)**

Prepare the pasta shells according to package directions. Drain and rinse.

Meanwhile, heat oil in a medium nonstick skillet over medium-high heat. Add onion and garlic; cook, stirring, until onion is tender, about 5 minutes. Stir in mushrooms and squash; cook, stirring, an additional 5 minutes. Remove from heat. Stir in olives and seasoning. Transfer vegetable mixture to mixing bowl. Set aside.

Pour pasta sauce into skillet. Heat sauce over medium heat until hot and bubbly; reduce heat to low. While sauce is heating, spoon vegetable mixture evenly into shells. Place stuffed shells in sauce. Cover skillet and cook until hot, about 7 minutes. Sprinkle with cheese, if desired, before serving.

Makes 4 servings

Helpful Hint

For a faster meal, combine pasta sauce with vegetables in skillet and serve it over other hot cooked pasta.

Per Serving:
259 Calories; 8g Protein; 5g Fat; 41g Carbohydrates; 1mg Cholesterol; 826mg Sodium; 5g Fiber.

Artichoke Spaghetti Sauce

½ cup chopped onion
1 to 2 cloves garlic, minced
¼ cup water
One 14½-ounce can diced
    tomatoes
One 14-ounce can artichoke
    hearts in water, drained
    and chopped
1 cup water
One 6-ounce can tomato paste
2 tablespoons sliced green
    olives (optional)
2 teaspoons brown sugar
2 teaspoons balsamic vinegar
1½ teaspoons dried oregano
    leaves
¼ teaspoon salt
¼ teaspoon freshly ground
    black pepper

In a 3-quart saucepan, cook onion and garlic in water over medium-high heat, stirring until onion is tender, about 5 minutes. Stir in remaining ingredients; mix well. Bring to a boil; reduce heat to low. Simmer for 15 to 20 minutes. Serve over hot cooked pasta of your choice.

Makes 5 cups; 10 servings

Per ½ Cup:
52 Calories; 2g Protein; 0 Fat;
12g Carbohydrates; 0 Cholesterol;
338mg Sodium; 3g Fiber.

Creamy Mushroom Stroganoff

10 ounces uncooked fettuccine
3 tablespoons butter
⅓ cup unbleached white flour
8 ounces fresh mushrooms,
**   sliced (about 3 cups), any**
**   variety**
¼ cup chopped shallots
3 to 4 cloves garlic, minced
1½ cups skim milk
½ cup dry white wine
2 tablespoons finely chopped
**   fresh parsley**
¼ to ½ teaspoon salt

Prepare the fettuccine according to package directions. Drain, rinse with hot water, and keep warm.

Meanwhile, in a medium nonstick skillet, melt the butter over medium heat. Stir in the flour until crumbly. Add mushrooms, shallots, and garlic. Cook until mixture is browned, stirring frequently, about 12 to 15 minutes.

Gradually add milk and wine. Stir constantly until mixture is smooth and comes to a boil; boil for 1 minute. Stir in parsley and salt. Serve immediately over fettuccine.

Makes 4 servings

Per Serving:
403 Calories; 13g Protein; 10g Fat; 62g Carbohydrates; 24mg Cholesterol; 278mg Sodium; 3g Fiber.

Broiled Eggplant Sandwiches

1 medium eggplant (about 20 ounces), cut lengthwise into six ½-inch-thick slices
1 tablespoon herb-flavored oil (see Helpful Hint)
6 whole wheat hoagie buns, split
6 tablespoons nonfat red wine vinaigrette
½ cup (about 2 ounces) shredded provolone cheese
1 medium tomato, thinly sliced
Assorted fresh greens

Preheat broiler.

Brush both sides of eggplant slices evenly with oil. Arrange eggplant on baking sheet. Broil 5 inches from heat until eggplant is tender and browned, about 15 minutes, turning once. Remove from broiler; set aside and keep warm.

Toast cut sides of buns under broiler, about 1 minute. Brush cut sides evenly with vinaigrette. Arrange eggplant, cheese, tomato, and greens evenly on buns. Serve immediately.

Makes 6 servings

VARIATION

If desired, top buns with eggplant and cheese, then broil to melt cheese before adding tomato and greens.

Helpful Hint

Herb and other flavored oils are available in supermarkets, natural food stores, and gourmet shops.

Per Serving:
294 Calories; 8g Protein; 9g Fat; 45g Carbohydrates; 6mg Cholesterol; 621mg Sodium; 4g Fiber.

Mock "Tuna" Salad

**One 15½-ounce can garbanzo
beans (chickpeas), drained**
**½ cup low-fat or regular
mayonnaise**
¼ cup diced onion
¼ cup diced celery
**1 hard-boiled egg, chopped
(optional)**
**Salt and/or hot pepper sauce to
taste**

Mash beans well with potato
masher or place beans in food
processor and process until beans
are the consistency of coarse meal.

In a medium bowl, combine
mashed or processed beans with
remaining ingredients. Serve as a
sandwich filling.

**Makes enough filling for 4
sandwiches; 4 servings**

Per Serving:
197 Calories; 5g Protein; 8g Fat;
27g Carbohydrates; 7mg Cholesterol; 450mg Sodium; 5g Fiber.

"Egg" Salad Sandwiches

8 ounces firm tofu, drained and diced or mashed
1 red bell pepper, finely chopped
1 small carrot, finely shredded
2 scallions, finely chopped
2 tablespoons nonfat or regular mayonnaise
1 tablespoon chopped fresh parsley
1 tablespoon finely chopped dill pickle
1 teaspoon prepared yellow mustard
¼ teaspoon salt
⅛ teaspoon pepper
8 slices whole wheat bread
Shredded lettuce and sliced tomatoes for garnish (optional)

In a medium bowl, combine all ingredients except bread and optional garnishes. Mix well. Adjust seasonings to taste.

Spread mixture evenly on 4 slices of bread. Top with lettuce and tomato slices, if desired, and remaining slices of bread.

Makes 4 sandwiches;
4 servings

Per Serving:
216 Calories; 10g Protein; 7g Fat; 32g Carbohydrates; 0 Cholesterol; 568mg Sodium; 5g Fiber.

Sloppy Joes

2 cups textured vegetable
protein (TVP) (see Helpful
Hint) granules or flakes
1¾ cups hot water
2 cloves garlic, minced
1 onion, chopped
1 green bell pepper, chopped
1 tablespoon olive oil
One 6-ounce can tomato paste
½ cup water
1 teaspoon dried oregano
leaves
¼ cup ketchup
1 tablespoon vinegar
¼ teaspoon cayenne pepper
1 teaspoon vegetarian
Worcestershire sauce (see
Helpful Hint)
1 tablespoon honey (optional)
Salt to taste (optional)
8 rolls or hamburger buns
Shredded lettuce

In a medium bowl, soak textured vegetable protein in water while preparing garlic, onion, and bell pepper.

Heat oil in a large skillet; add garlic, onion, and bell pepper. Drain textured vegetable protein and add to skillet. Cook, stirring, for about 3 minutes.

Meanwhile, in a separate bowl, mix tomato paste with water, oregano, ketchup, vinegar, cayenne pepper, Worcestershire sauce, and honey, if desired. Stir into skillet mixture.

Bring to a boil. Add salt to taste, if desired. Sauce should be thick but spreadable. Add a little more water if needed.

Spoon sauce on bottom half of roll, pile on lettuce, and top with remaining roll half.

**Makes 8 sandwiches;
8 servings**

Helpful Hint

Textured vegetable protein, also called TVP, is a dehydrated soy product with a texture that resembles meat. It is sold as granules, flakes and chunks, plain or flavored, in natural food stores.

Vegetarian versions of Worcestershire sauce are available in supermarkets and natural food stores.

Per Serving:
217 Calories; 14g Protein; 3g Fat;
32g Carbohydrates; 0 Cholesterol;
462mg Sodium; 4g Fiber.

Terry's Eggplant Sandwich

*Using leftover cooked rice would make this tasty sandwich
an even faster meal.*

**1 cup uncooked quick-cooking
     brown rice**
1 tablespoon olive oil
1 eggplant, peeled and chopped
1 onion, chopped
2 cloves garlic, minced
**One 16-ounce can whole toma-
     toes, chopped, undrained**
**Salt and freshly ground black
     pepper to taste**
¼ teaspoon red pepper flakes
4 large pita rounds, cut in half

Cook rice according to package
directions. Set aside.

Meanwhile, in a wok or large
skillet, heat oil. Add eggplant and
stir-fry until eggplant shrinks, 5 to
10 minutes. Add onion and garlic
and stir-fry a few minutes more.
Stir in tomatoes, salt, pepper, and
red pepper flakes.

Cover and let simmer until
eggplant reaches desired tender-
ness, about 5 minutes. Stir in rice.
Fill pita pockets with rice-eggplant
mixture.

**Makes 4 sandwiches;
4 servings**

VARIATION

*Omit rice and pita bread; serve
eggplant mixture over thin spaghetti, vermicelli, or linguine.*

Per Sandwich:
434 Calories; 11g Protein; 5g Fat;
83g Carb; 0 Cholesterol; 758mg
Sodium; 9g Fiber.

Open-Faced Veggie Sandwiches

3 tablespoons low-fat or regular mayonnaise
4 slices pumpernickel bread
1 cup shredded, unpeeled zucchini
1 cup sliced fresh mushrooms
¼ cup sliced scallions
Salt and freshly ground black pepper to taste
4 tomato slices, cut in half
4 slices (1 ounce each) low-fat or regular Monterey Jack cheese or other favorite cheese

Spread mayonnaise evenly on bread slices. Set aside.

In a medium mixing bowl, combine the zucchini, mushrooms, and scallions. Season to taste with salt and pepper. Spoon mixture evenly over prepared pumpernickel slices.

Place sandwiches under broiler, 4 inches from heat. Broil until zucchini begins to brown, about 5 minutes. Remove from oven. Top each sandwich evenly with tomato slices and cheese. Return to broiler until cheese melts, about 1 minute. Serve immediately.

**Makes 4 sandwiches;
4 servings**

Per Serving:
184 Calories; 10g Protein; 8g Fat; 20g Carbohydrates; 8mg Cholesterol; 672mg Sodium; 3g Fiber.

Tempeh Reuben Sandwiches

SAUCE:

**1 teaspoon arrowroot powder
(see Helpful Hint) or cornstarch**

1 teaspoon cold water

⅓ cup vegetable broth or water

**4 teaspoons stone-ground
mustard**

**1½ teaspoons mellow miso (see
Helpful Hint)**

1 teaspoon fresh lemon juice

SANDWICHES:

2 teaspoons canola oil

**8 ounces five-grain or regular
tempeh (see Helpful Hint)**

½ cup vegetable broth or water

**12 slices rye or pumpernickel
bread, toasted**

**Fresh lettuce leaves or other
greens**

**1½ cups well-drained
sauerkraut**

6 scallions, thinly sliced

**1 teaspoon finely chopped fresh
dill**

For the sauce, in a small mixing bowl, combine the arrowroot or cornstarch and cold water; stir until smooth. Whisk in the remaining sauce ingredients until smooth; set aside.

For the sandwiches, heat the oil in a medium nonstick skillet over medium heat. Brown tempeh in skillet, turning once, about 4 minutes. Add vegetable broth or water; cover skillet. Cook until all liquid is absorbed, turning tempeh once or twice, about 8 minutes.

While tempeh is cooking, toast bread slices and prepare lettuce, sauerkraut, scallions, and dill.

Remove skillet from heat. Cut tempeh crosswise into thin slices. Pour sauce into skillet with tempeh slices. Return to heat, stirring gently and constantly, until sauce thickens, about 30 seconds.

Layer lettuce, tempeh, sauerkraut, scallions, and dill evenly on 6 toast slices. Top with remaining toast slices. Serve immediately.

**Makes 6 sandwiches;
6 servings**

Per Serving:
271 Calories; 11g Protein; 5g Fat;
45g Carbohydrates; 0 Cholesterol;
925mg Sodium; 7g Fiber.

Helpful Hints

Arrowroot powder is the ground root of the arrowroot plant, used for thickening. It can substitute for cornstarch measure for measure. Arrowroot powder is available in natural food stores, specialty stores, and some supermarkets.

Miso is fermented soybean paste used as a condiment, particularly in Japanese cuisine. The darker varieties are more pronounced in flavor than the lighter, or "mellow," varieties. Miso may contain other grains, such as barley, in addition to soybeans.

Tempeh is a high-protein soy food with a rich taste and meaty texture that is often used as a meat substitute. It is a cake of fermented whole soybeans, usually sold in eight-ounce packages in natural food stores and in some supermarkets. Tempeh is available plain, flavored, and as a combination of soybeans and other grains.

Pesto Ricotta Sandwiches

Wonderful Mediterranean flavors—pesto, ricotta, sun-dried tomatoes, and garlic—all wrapped up in one sandwich, and on the table in twenty minutes.

1 cup part-skim ricotta cheese
2 tablespoons prepared basil pesto
2 teaspoons finely chopped sun-dried tomatoes in oil, drained and patted dry
1 clove garlic, minced
Freshly ground black pepper to taste
6 slices Italian bread, toasted
1 medium tomato, sliced
1 cup shredded fresh spinach

Preheat broiler.

In a small mixing bowl, combine the cheese, pesto, sun-dried tomatoes, garlic, and pepper; mix well with fork. Spread mixture evenly on toast slices. Top evenly with tomato slices.

Place sandwiches under broiler with surface of sandwiches 4 inches from the heat. Broil until hot and browned on edges, about 5 minutes. Top sandwiches evenly with spinach. Serve immediately.

Makes 6 open-faced sandwiches; 6 servings

Per Serving:
159 Calories; 8g Protein; 6g Fat; 18g Carbohydrates; 13mg Cholesterol; 253mg Sodium; 1g Fiber.

Portobello Muffuletta

One 1-pound round sourdough bread loaf
1 tablespoon red wine vinegar
2 teaspoons Dijon mustard
2 teaspoon olive oil
¼ teaspoon sugar
¼ teaspoon salt
¼ teaspoon freshly ground black pepper
6 ounces fresh portobello mushroom caps
1 cup torn fresh romaine lettuce
¼ cup chopped sun-dried tomatoes in oil, drained
2 ounces provolone cheese, sliced
1 medium fresh tomato, sliced
1 small onion, sliced

Slice off the top ⅓ of the bread loaf and set aside. Pull out center of bread with your hands, leaving a 1-inch shell around outer edge and on bottom. Set aside hollowed-out bread loaf, and reserve the center of the loaf for another use.

Preheat broiler.

In a 1-cup measure or small bowl, combine vinegar, mustard, oil, sugar, salt, and pepper; whisk until smooth. Brush half of mustard mixture evenly over tops of mushrooms. Broil mushrooms about 4 inches from heat until lightly browned, about 5 minutes.

Brush remaining mustard mixture evenly over inside of hollowed-out loaf. Layer lettuce on bottom and up sides of loaf. Layer evenly with sun-dried tomatoes, mushrooms, cheese, tomato, and onion.

Top filled loaf with reserved top crust; press down firmly with hands. Cut into 6 wedges to serve.

Makes 6 sandwiches;
6 servings

Helpful Hint

This sandwich packs well for picnics. Prepare the muffuletta in advance, wrap it tightly in plastic wrap, and refrigerate. Slice just before serving.

Per Serving:
278 Calories; 10g Protein; 7g Fat; 43g Carbohydrates; 6mg Cholesterol; 653mg Sodium; 6g Fiber.

Grilled Zucchini Sandwiches

1 medium zucchini (about 12 ounces)
Nonstick cooking spray
2 slices red onion, separated into rings
3 tablespoons Dijon mustard
8 slices whole grain bread
¼ cup (1 ounce) shredded pepper cheese
1 cup alfalfa sprouts

Cut zucchini lengthwise into 4 slices; cut each slice in half crosswise. Spray a large nonstick skillet with nonstick cooking spray. Heat skillet over medium heat. Add zucchini, and cook until browned, turning once, about 3 minutes per side. Remove zucchini from skillet; set aside.

Add onion to the same skillet, and cook, stirring, until soft, about 2 minutes. Remove from skillet; set aside. Wipe skillet clean with paper towel.

Spread mustard evenly on one side of each slice of bread. Layer zucchini, onion, cheese, and sprouts evenly among 4 slices of bread. Top with remaining bread slices.

Heat skillet over medium heat. Spray with nonstick cooking spray. Grill sandwiches, one or two at a time, until lightly browned, turning once, about 2 minutes per side. Serve hot.

Makes 4 sandwiches;
4 servings

Per Serving:
191 Calories; 8g Protein; 6g Fat; 27g Carbohydrates; 6mg Cholesterol; 587mg Sodium; 5g Fiber.

Broccoli-Cauliflower Luncheon Salad

The next time you make couscous, make enough so that you have leftovers for this recipe too.

5 cups water
2 cups fresh broccoli florets
1½ cups fresh cauliflower
    florets
One 15½-ounce can red kidney
    beans, rinsed and drained
¼ cup sliced scallions
¼ cup chopped carrot
2 tablespoons olive oil
2 tablespoons cider vinegar
1 tablespoon Dijon mustard
1 clove garlic, minced
⅛ teaspoon freshly ground
    black pepper
2 cups chilled cooked couscous
    (see Helpful Hint)

Bring water to a boil in a 3-quart saucepan over high heat. Add broccoli and cauliflower. Cook about 1 minute; drain, and place immediately into a bowl of ice water to cool.

In a large mixing bowl, combine beans, scallions, and carrot. Drain broccoli and cauliflower well, then add to bean mixture. Mix well. Set aside.

In a small mixing bowl, combine oil, vinegar, mustard, garlic, and pepper; whisk until smooth. Add mixture to vegetables; toss to coat. Serve vegetable salad over chilled couscous.

Makes 4 servings

Helpful Hint

Couscous is steamed, dried, and crushed durum wheat common in Middle Eastern cuisine. The tiny "grain" has a mild flavor, cooks up quickly, and can be used in just about any recipe calling for a bed of rice or other grain. Couscous can be purchased in natural food stores and in supermarkets.

VARIATION

Omit couscous and serve salad over a bed of lettuce.

Per Serving:
271 Calories; 11g Protein; 8g Fat;42 G Carbohydrates; 0 Cholesterol; 499mg Sodium; 8g Fiber.

Vegetable Tortellini Salad

This quick salad—twenty minutes from stove to table—makes a hearty meal.

One 9-ounce package fresh cheese tortellini
1 cup halved cherry tomatoes
2 medium carrots, sliced (about ¾ cup)
½ medium green bell pepper, seeded and cut into strips
⅓ cup nonfat Italian dressing
¼ cup sliced scallions
2 tablespoons freshly grated Parmesan cheese

Prepare the tortellini according to package directions. While tortellini is cooking, prepare vegetables.

When tortellini is tender, drain. Rinse with cold water; drain again. In a large mixing bowl, combine tortellini with remaining ingredients, except cheese; toss to combine. Sprinkle salad with Parmesan cheese.

Makes 4 to 6 servings

Per Serving:
134 Calories; 6g Protein; 3g Fat; 21g Carbohydrates; 15mg Cholesterol; 400mg Sodium; 2g Fiber.

Greek Salad

SALAD:

2 cups torn fresh spinach
   leaves
3 medium tomatoes, cut into
   thin wedges
1 medium cucumber, peeled
   and sliced
1 medium green bell pepper,
   seeded and cut into thin
   strips
1 medium yellow or red bell
   pepper, cut into thin strips
1 medium zucchini, sliced
2 tablespoons sliced green
   onion
2 ounces feta cheese, crumbled
¼ cup chopped kalamata olives
1 tablespoons finely chopped
   fresh basil

DRESSING:

¼ cup fresh lemon juice
2 tablespoons olive oil
2 teaspoons dried parsley
1 teaspoon dried oregano
1 teaspoon salt
1 teaspoon freshly ground
   black pepper

In a large salad or mixing bowl,
combine all salad ingredients; toss
lightly to combine.

In a 1-cup measure or small
bowl, combine dressing ingredients; whisk well. Drizzle dressing
over salad; toss lightly to coat.

Makes 6 to 8 servings

Per Serving:
116 Calories; 4g Protein; 8g Fat;
10g Carbohydrates; 8mg Cholesterol; 527mg Sodium; 3g Fiber.

Taco Salad

4 large flour tortillas
Nonstick cooking spray
One 15½-ounce can pinto
    beans, rinsed and drained
½ cup chopped yellow or green
    bell pepper
⅓ cup chopped onion
2 tablespoons tamari (see
    Helpful Hint) or regular soy
    sauce
2 cloves garlic, minced
1 teaspoon chili powder
½ teaspoon ground cumin
4 cups torn fresh salad greens
1 medium tomato, chopped
½ cup shredded cheddar
    cheese
Salsa, plain yogurt, sliced black
    olives, and chopped avo-
    cado for garnish (optional)

Preheat oven to 350°F.

To make shells for salad, spray both sides of tortillas with non-stick cooking spray. Gently press each tortilla into a 4-ounce custard cup or small ovenproof bowl. Bake for 15 minutes, until shells are crisp.

While shells are baking, spray a medium nonstick skillet with nonstick cooking spray. Add beans, pepper, onion, tamari or soy sauce, garlic, chili powder, and cumin. Cook over medium heat, stirring constantly, until heated through, about 5 minutes.

Remove baked tortilla shells from cups or bowls. Place 1 cup of greens in each tortilla shell. Spoon bean mixture evenly into shells. Top with chopped tomato and shredded cheese. Garnish with salsa, yogurt, olives, and avocado as desired.

Makes 4 servings

Helpful Hint

Tamari is a variety of Japanese soy sauce that is dark and rich tasting, and usually wheat-free. It is available in supermarkets and natural food stores.

Per Serving:
304 Calories; 15g Protein; 9g Fat; 42g Carbohydrates; 15mg Cholesterol; 1,245mg Sodium; 7g Fiber.

Autumn Salad with Low-Fat Vinaigrette

VINAIGRETTE:

1 teaspoon Dijon mustard
**2 tablespoons minced garlic, or
to taste**
¼ cup apple cider vinegar
2 tablespoons fresh lemon juice
2 tablespoons olive oil
2 tablespoons tomato juice
**1 teaspoon miso (see Helpful
Hint) or 1 tablespoon soy
sauce**
**¼ teaspoon black pepper or
cayenne pepper**

SALAD:

**¼ cup cooked or canned beans
of your choice**
½ cup thinly sliced cucumber
½ cup diced tomatoes
**1 teaspoon drained capers (see
Helpful Hints)**
¼ cup diced red bell pepper
**¼ cup fresh or frozen (thawed)
corn kernels**
2 lettuce leaves

In a small bowl or blender, combine all vinaigrette ingredients and whisk or blend well. If using miso instead of soy sauce, blend until miso is dissolved.

For the salad, combine beans, cucumber, and ¼ cup of the vinaigrette in a medium bowl. If you have time, cover and let mixture marinate in refrigerator for about 1 hour.

Add tomatoes, capers, bell pepper, and corn; toss well to coat. Place lettuce on two salad plates; spoon bean mixture onto lettuce. Add more vinaigrette to taste.

Makes 2 servings

Helpful Hints

Miso is fermented soybean paste that is used as a condiment and a seasoning. It comes in several varieties; the lighter "mellow" varieties tend to be milder in flavor than the darker ones. Miso is available in natural food stores and Asian groceries.

Capers are the buds of a small Mediterranean shrub that are pickled or dried and salted and used as a condiment and seasoning. They are available in supermarkets and gourmet food stores.

Per Serving:
105 Calories; 2g Protein; 3g Fat;
15g Carbohydrates; 0 Cholesterol;
30mg Sodium; 4g Fiber.

Aztec Platter

The grain from the quinoa plant was a mainstay of the diet of the ancient Aztecs. Aztec Platter features a salad made with this ancient grain, which is now widely available in supermarkets.

QUINOA-CORN SALAD:

2 cups water
1 cup quinoa, well-rinsed (see Helpful Hints)
½ cup cooked fresh or frozen corn kernels, thawed
Juice of 1 lemon
2 to 3 scallions, minced
1 tablespoon olive oil
Salt and freshly ground black pepper to taste

BEAN SALAD:

1½ cups cooked or canned pinto, kidney, or Anasazi beans (see Helpful Hints)
1 heaping cup finely diced ripe tomatoes
1 tablespoon balsamic or cider vinegar
¼ cup chopped fresh parsley
Salt and freshly ground black pepper to taste

GARNISHES:

Pumpkin seeds
Black olives
Red pepper or pimientos, cut into narrow strips about 1½ inches long

For the quinoa-corn salad, bring water to a boil in a small, heavy saucepan. Add quinoa and simmer gently, covered, until water is absorbed, about 15 minutes. Fluff with a fork, then let cool to room temperature. Transfer to a mixing bowl and combine with remaining quinoa-corn salad ingredients.

In a separate bowl, combine all bean salad ingredients and toss together.

Transfer quinoa-corn salad onto center of platter. Make a well in center about 5 inches in diameter. Mound bean salad into well. Sprinkle with pumpkin seeds. Arrange olives and strips of pepper or pimientos around rim of platter.

Makes 6 servings

Per Serving:
223 Calories; 8g Protein; 5g Fat; 37g Carbohydrates; 0 Cholesterol; 292mg Sodium; 8g Fiber.

Helpful Hints

Quinoa is a high-protein grain originally from South America. It is tiny, round, and mild in flavor. It cooks up quickly and can be used as a substitute for rice, couscous, or almost any other grain. Quinoa is available in natural food stores and in some supermarkets. Be sure to rinse it very well before cooking to remove a natural but bitter-tasting resin that coats the grains.

Anasazi beans are red and white beans with a sweet flavor. Look for them in gourmet food shops, natural food stores, and some supermarkets.

Peppers Stuffed with Couscous Salad

6 whole bell peppers, any color
⅓ cup diced green bell peppers
⅓ cup diced red bell peppers
⅓ cup diced yellow bell peppers
⅓ cup chopped scallions
⅓ cup diced zucchini
⅓ cup diced yellow squash
1½ cups cooked couscous, cooled (see Helpful Hints)
3 tablespoons rice vinegar (see Helpful Hints)
1 teaspoon canola oil
⅓ cup chopped fresh Italian parsley
1 tablespoon fresh lime juice
Salt and freshly ground black pepper to taste

Slice off tops of whole bell peppers; core, seed, wash, and drain. Slice off enough of bottom of peppers, making sure not to slice through, so they sit on a platter without falling over.

In a mixing bowl, combine diced peppers, scallions, zucchini, yellow squash, and couscous. In a separate bowl, combine vinegar, oil, parsley, lime juice, salt, and pepper. Add parsley mixture to couscous mixture; toss well.

Spoon couscous filling into peppers, cover with plastic wrap or waxed paper, and refrigerate until serving time.

Makes 6 servings

Helpful Hints

Couscous is steamed, dried, and crushed durum wheat common in Middle Eastern cuisine. The tiny "grain" has a mild flavor, cooks up quickly, and can be used in just about any recipe calling for a bed of rice or other grain. Couscous can be purchased in natural food stores and in supermarkets.

Rice vinegar is a mild vinegar made from rice that is a popular seasoning in Japanese cuisine. It is excellent in sauces and salads. Rice vinegar is available in supermarkets and in natural food stores.

Per Serving:
78 Calories; 2g Protein; 1g Fat; 15g Carbohydrates; 0 Cholesterol; 7mg Sodium; 3g Fiber.

Easy Vegetable Soup

Frozen vegetables are a high-quality, time-saving alternative to cutting up fresh vegetables. With a wide assortment of vegetable mixtures available, you can tailor this supereasy recipe to suit your tastes.

1 tablespoon butter

One 10-ounce package frozen seasoning mix (onions, green and red bell peppers, parsley) or about ¼ cup each: onion, celery, green bell pepper, and red bell pepper, plus fresh parsley to taste

One 16-ounce bag frozen mixed vegetables with potatoes

One 10-ounce package frozen mixed vegetables with peas and carrots

1 cup coarsely chopped cabbage

2⅔ cups spicy vegetable juice

2 cups water or vegetable broth

1 teaspoon salt

Melt butter in a 6-quart pot over medium-high heat. Add frozen seasoning mix. Cook, stirring, for 5 minutes. Add 16-ounce bag of mixed vegetables. Cook, stirring, until vegetables are nearly tender, about 10 minutes. Add remaining frozen vegetables and cabbage. Cook, stirring, until cabbage begins to soften, about 3 minutes.

Stir in remaining ingredients. Bring to a boil over high heat. Reduce heat to medium-low. Cover; simmer until vegetables are tender and flavors are blended, about 10 minutes.

Makes 6 servings

Per Serving:
68 Calories; 2g Protein; 2g Fat; 11g Carbohydrates; 5mg Cholesterol; 793mg Sodium; 2g Fiber.

Smoky White Bean Soup

Smoked gouda cheese gives this soup the same traditional, comforting flavor that comes from smoked bacon in meat-based cuisine.

1 pound russet potatoes, peeled and cut into ½-inch cubes (about 3 cups)

3 cups water or vegetable broth

1 medium onion, chopped

Three 15½-ounce cans great northern beans, rinsed and drained

1 cup 1 percent or skim milk

1 teaspoon ground cumin

⅛ to ¼ teaspoon cayenne pepper

3 ounces smoked gouda cheese, shredded (about 1 cup)

Salt and freshly ground black pepper to taste

Finely chopped red and green bell pepper or seeded tomato as garnish (optional)

In a 6-quart pot, combine potatoes, 2 cups water or broth, and onion. Cover. Bring to a boil over high heat. Reduce heat to medium. Simmer until potatoes are tender, about 10 minutes.

Process potatoes, onions, and cooking water or broth in batches in a blender or food processor until smooth. Return mixture to pot. Stir in remaining 1 cup water or broth, beans, milk, cumin, and cayenne pepper. Simmer over medium heat until hot, about 5 minutes.

Remove pot from heat. Stir in cheese. Add salt and pepper to taste. Garnish individual servings with chopped bell pepper or tomato if desired.

Makes 8 servings

Per Serving:
288 Calories; 17g Protein; 4g Fat; 48g Carbohydrates; 13mg Cholesterol; 112mg Sodium; 9g Fiber.

African Sweet Potato Stew

The mixture of sweet potatoes, tomatoes, and peanut butter is a common flavor combination in African cuisine.

1 tablespoon olive oil

1 large onion, chopped (about 2 cups)

2 cups chopped cabbage (see Helpful Hint)

3 to 4 cloves garlic, minced

One 18-ounce can sweet potatoes, drained and chopped

One 14½-ounce can tomato wedges or diced tomatoes, undrained

1½ cups tomato juice

¾ cup apple juice

1 to 2 teaspoons grated fresh ginger root

¼ to ½ teaspoon red pepper flakes

2 cups frozen cut green beans

⅓ cup natural peanut butter

Heat oil in a large skillet over medium-high heat. Add onion; cook, stirring, until tender, about 5 minutes. Mix in cabbage and garlic; cook, stirring, until cabbage is tender-crisp, about 5 minutes.

Stir in sweet potatoes, tomatoes, tomato juice, apple juice, ginger, and red pepper flakes. Reduce heat to medium-low; cover. Simmer until hot and bubbling, about 6 minutes.

Stir in green beans and simmer, uncovered, for 5 minutes. Stir in peanut butter until well blended and hot, about 1 minute. Serve stew with crusty bread and a salad, or spoon it over rice or mashed potatoes.

Makes 6 servings

Helpful Hint

To save time, use packaged cabbage slaw mix instead of chopping up a head of cabbage.

Per Serving:
261 Calories; 8g Protein; 9g Fat; 40g Carbohydrates; 0 Cholesterol; 425mg Sodium; 8g Fiber.

Vegetable Stew with Dumplings

STEW:

1 tablespoon oil
2 stalks celery, cut into ½-inch slices
1 small onion, cut into 8 wedges
3 cups vegetable broth or water
One 1-pound bag frozen mixed vegetables
1 bay leaf
½ teaspoon dried thyme
¼ teaspoons salt
⅓ cup unbleached white flour
½ cup cold water

DUMPLINGS:

1½ cups unbleached white flour
2 teaspoons baking powder
½ teaspoon salt
1 teaspoon dried parsley flakes
¼ teaspoon dried dill
⅔ cup skim milk
1 egg, slightly beaten
1 tablespoon canola oil

For the stew, heat oil in a 2-quart saucepan over medium heat. Cook the celery and onion, stirring, until tender-crisp, about 3 minutes. Stir in broth or water, vegetables, bay leaf, thyme, and salt. Bring to a boil over high heat. Reduce heat to medium-low; simmer for 5 minutes.

Meanwhile, for the dumplings, in a medium mixing bowl, combine 1½ cups flour, baking powder, salt, parsley, and dill. Add milk, egg, and oil; mix well. Set aside.

In a 2-cup measure or a small bowl, combine ⅓ cup flour and cold water; whisk until smooth. Gradually stir flour mixture into stew. Bring to a boil over high heat. Drop dumpling batter by heaping tablespoons into stew. Reduce heat to medium-low; cover. Simmer until dumplings are no longer doughy, about 10 minutes.

Makes 4 servings

Per Serving:
378 Calories; 13g Protein; 9g Fat; 64g Carbohydrates; 54mg Cholesterol; 821mg Sodium; 5g Fiber.

Pesto Vegetable Soup

2 teaspoons garlic-flavored oil (see Helpful Hint) or regular olive oil
1 medium onion, cut into quarters and sliced
6 cups vegetable broth or water
One 16-ounce bag frozen mixed vegetables
One 15½-ounce can navy beans or great northern beans, rinsed and drained
2 cups uncooked rotini (about 6 ounces)
¼ cup prepared basil pesto

In a 6-quart pot, heat oil over medium heat. Add onion; cook, stirring, until golden brown, about 10 minutes. Add a small amount of broth or water if necessary to prevent sticking.

Stir in broth or water, vegetables, and beans. Bring to a boil over high heat. Stir in rotini. Reduce heat to medium. Simmer until rotini is tender, about 10 minutes, stirring occasionally. Stir in pesto just before serving.

Makes 6 servings

Helpful Hint

Garlic and other flavored oils are available in most supermarkets and natural food stores.

Per Serving:
357 Calories; 14g Protein; 8g Fat; 58g Carbohydrates; 2mg Cholesterol; 545mg Sodium; 7g Fiber.

Eggplant-Chickpea Stew

Nonstick cooking spray
1 medium eggplant (about 20 ounces), cut into ½-inch slices
1 tablespoon garlic-flavored oil (see Helpful Hint)
1 medium onion, chopped
Two 14½-ounce cans tomato wedges, undrained
One 15½-ounce can chickpeas (garbanzo beans), rinsed and drained
½ teaspoon fennel seed, slightly crushed
¼ teaspoon salt
Freshly ground black pepper to taste
Chopped fresh parsley for garnish (optional)

Preheat broiler. Spray a large baking sheet with nonstick cooking spray. Place eggplant slices on baking sheet, and broil about 5 inches from heat until browned and nearly tender, about 10 minutes, turning once. Cut into cubes.

While eggplant is broiling, heat oil in a large nonstick skillet over medium heat. Add onion; cook, stirring, until tender, about 5 minutes. Stir in tomato wedges, chickpeas, fennel, salt, and pepper. Add eggplant, and simmer for 10 minutes to blend flavors, stirring occasionally. Garnish individual servings with parsley, if desired.

Makes 4 servings

Helpful Hint

Garlic and other flavored oils are available in most supermarkets and natural food stores.

Per Serving:
262 Calories; 9g Protein; 5g Fat; 49g Carbohydrates; 0 Cholesterol; 902mg Sodium; 13g Fiber.

Corn and Potato Chowder

1 teaspoon safflower oil
2 teaspoons dry sherry or
    water
1¼ cups finely chopped onion
1 cup thinly sliced carrots
2 stalks celery with leaves,
    thinly sliced
1 bay leaf
2 cups cubed red potatoes
1 cup vegetable broth
1 cup skim milk
1 cup fresh or frozen (thawed)
    corn kernels
Cayenne pepper to taste
Nonfat plain yogurt for garnish
    (optional)

In a large, heavy saucepan, heat oil and sherry or water until bubbling. Add onion and cook, 5 minutes, stirring frequently to prevent browning. (If mixture appears dry, add 1 to 2 table-spoons more sherry or water.)

Add carrots, celery, bay leaf, potatoes, and broth. Cover pan, bring to a boil, and cook over medium heat until potatoes are tender, about 10 to 15 minutes. Add milk and corn and simmer until corn is tender, about 3 minutes. Remove and discard bay leaf.

Puree 1 cup of the soup in a food processor or blender, then return to the pot. Season with cayenne pepper. If desired, garnish individual servings with a dollop of yogurt.

Makes 4 servings

Per Serving:
196 Calories; 5g Protein; 1g Fat; 39g Carbohydrates; 1mg Choles-terol; 1mg Sodium; 7g Fiber.

Thick 'n' Spicy Tortellini Stew

Prepared fresh pasta is a godsend when you need to get a meal on the table fast. Here, it's the basis of a hearty stew.

One 9-ounce package fresh cheese tortellini
½ cup chopped onion
1 medium red bell pepper, seeded and chopped
1 medium yellow bell pepper, seeded and chopped
⅓ cup sliced celery
2 cloves garlic, minced
2 teaspoons canola oil
5½ cups vegetable broth
2 cups chunky salsa
One 12-ounce can tomato paste
½ teaspoon ground cumin
Chopped fresh cilantro (optional)

Prepare the tortellini according to package directions. While the tortellini cooks, sauté the onion, bell peppers, celery, and garlic in oil, stirring, in a 4-quart saucepan over medium heat until the vegetables are tender-crisp, about 2 to 4 minutes.

Stir in the broth, salsa, tomato paste, and cumin. Simmer for 10 minutes. Drain the tortellini and add to the saucepan. Simmer until heated through. Sprinkle individual servings with chopped cilantro, if desired.

Makes 6 servings

Per Serving:
310 Calories; 12g Protein; 6g Fat; 57g Carbohydrates; 9mg Cholesterol; 2,345mg Sodium; 5g Fiber.

Creamy Potato Soup

You can get this lovely cream of potato soup on the table in thirty minutes.

8 red potatoes, unpeeled, cut into ½-inch cubes (about 3 cups)

2 cups water

1 medium leek, chopped (white part only) or ½ cup chopped onion

½ cup chopped carrot

½ teaspoon salt

¼ teaspoon summer savory

⅛ teaspoon freshly ground black pepper

1½ cups 1 percent milk

3 tablespoons unbleached white flour

In a 3-quart saucepan, combine the potatoes, water, leek or onion, carrot, salt, summer savory, and pepper. Bring to a boil over medium-high heat. Reduce heat to medium-low, cover, and simmer until potatoes are tender, about 12 minutes.

In a 2-cup measure or small bowl, combine milk and flour; stir until smooth. Increase heat under saucepan to medium-high. Stir flour mixture into soup. Bring to a boil; boil for 1 minute, stirring occasionally.

Makes 6 servings

VARIATION

For a heartier soup, sprinkle each serving with 1 to 2 tablespoons shredded cheese of your choice.

Per Serving:
128 Calories; 4g Protein; 1g Fat; 26g Carbohydrates; 2mg Cholesterol; 222mg Sodium; 2g Fiber.

Four-Bean Chili

No one ever has enough chili recipes. Here's one that features four different types of beans.

2 cups chopped red or yellow bell pepper or a mixture
1 cup chopped onion
2 cloves garlic, minced
2 teaspoons olive oil
4 cups vegetable broth (see Helpful Hints)
One 15½-ounce can butter beans, rinsed and drained
One 15-ounce can adzuki beans, rinsed and drained (see Helpful Hints)
One 15-ounce can pinto beans, rinsed and drained
One 15-ounce can black beans, rinsed and drained
One 4½-ounce can chopped green chile peppers
2 teaspoons chili powder
2 teaspoons ground cumin
½ teaspoon dried oregano leaves
¼ teaspoon red pepper flakes
Nonfat plain yogurt (optional)

In a 4-quart saucepan, cook peppers, onion, and garlic in oil, stirring, over medium heat until vegetables are tender-crisp, about 2 to 4 minutes. Stir in all remaining ingredients except yogurt. Bring to a boil over high heat. Reduce heat to medium-low. Cover and simmer for 10 minutes to blend flavors. Top individual servings with a dollop of yogurt, if desired.

Makes 6 servings

Helpful Hints

For a thicker chili, reduce the vegetable broth by one or two cups, depending on desired thickness.

Adzuki beans, also called aduki and azuki beans, are small, sweet beans popular in Japanese cuisine. They are available in natural food stores and Asian markets.

Per Serving:
407 Calories; 21g Protein; 3g Fat; 74g Carbohydrates; 0 Cholesterol; 110mg Sodium; 15g Fiber.

Gingered Carrot Soup

1 cup chopped onions
4 cups vegetable broth
2 heads garlic, cloves separated but unpeeled, tied in a cheesecloth bag
1 cup chopped carrots
1 cup diced white potatoes
⅓ cup blanched almonds
2 teaspoons grated ginger root
1 tablespoon frozen orange juice concentrate, thawed
1 tablespoon honey
Salt and freshly ground black pepper to taste

Place onions, broth, garlic, carrots, and potatoes in a large soup pot or pressure cooker over medium-high heat. Cover and bring to a boil. Reduce heat and simmer 20 minutes. (If using a pressure cooker, bring to 15 pounds pressure and cook 10 minutes; bring down pressure by the cold water method and remove lid.)

Let cool slightly, remove garlic, add almonds, and puree soup in a blender or food processor. Stir in remaining ingredients and serve.

Makes 4 servings

Helpful Hint

For a richer-tasting soup, let sit in refrigerator overnight so flavors can develop.

Per Serving:
156 Calories; 3g Protein; 6g Fat;
21g Carbohydrates; 0 Cholesterol;
17mg Sodium; 4g Fiber.

Parsley and Yellow Potato Soup

4 cups vegetable broth
2 cups chopped Yellow Finn, Yukon Gold, or other yellow potatoes
1 medium onion, finely chopped
1 cup sliced leek (white part only)
1 teaspoon salt
¼ teaspoon ground white pepper
¼ cup chopped fresh parsley
2 tablespoons chopped fresh chives

In a 4-quart saucepan, combine broth, potatoes, onion, and leek. Bring to a boil over high heat. Reduce heat to low, cover, and simmer until vegetables are tender, about 10 minutes.

In a food processor or blender, process mixture until smooth. Season with salt and pepper. Garnish individual servings with parsley and chives. Serve immediately.

Makes 4 servings

Per Serving:
161 Calories; 3g Protein; 0 Fat;
36g Carbohydrates; 0 Cholesterol;
640mg Sodium; 3g Fiber.

Spicy Southwestern Black Bean Soup

If you're shy when it comes to spicy food, use just half of the chile peppers called for in this robust soup.

1½ teaspoons olive oil
1 large onion, coarsely chopped
One 4-ounce can chopped
    green chile peppers
2 cloves garlic, minced
Two 15½-ounce cans black
    beans with liquid
2 teaspoons chili powder, or to
    taste
1 teaspoon ground cumin
1 teaspoon fresh lemon juice, or
    to taste
One 28-ounce can diced
    tomatoes, undrained
1 cup water as needed to thin
    soup
¼ cup chopped fresh cilantro

In a large soup pot or Dutch oven, heat oil. Add onion and cook, stirring, over medium-high heat until onion is transparent, about 3 minutes. Add chiles and garlic; cook, stirring, 2 minutes more.

Add all remaining ingredients except cilantro; stir and simmer about 10 minutes. Stir in cilantro just before serving.

Makes 6 servings

Per Serving:
199 Calories; 11g Protein; 1g Fat;
37g Carbohydrates; 0 Cholesterol;
366mg Sodium; 8g Fiber.

Potato-Kale Stew

Pressure cookers vastly reduce the amount of time in the kitchen. Use a pressure cooker for this recipe for super-quick preparation.

1 tablespoon olive oil
1 yellow onion, sliced
2 cloves garlic, minced
3 to 4 medium potatoes, cut into 1-inch chunks
One 14½-ounce can diced tomatoes, undrained
One 15½-ounce can garbanzo beans, undrained
1 tablespoon dried basil
4 to 8 ounces kale, torn into large pieces
Cooked rice or other cooked grain (optional)
Freshly grated Parmesan cheese to taste (optional)

In a pressure cooker, heat oil and add onion; cook, stirring, over medium-high heat 3 minutes. Add garlic and potatoes and cook, stirring, about 1 minute.

Add tomatoes with juice, beans with liquid, and basil; stir well. Bring to a boil; arrange kale on top. Lock on lid and bring to pressure over high heat.

Turn down heat just enough to maintain pressure. Cook at pressure for 3 minutes and remove from heat. Bring down pressure by placing cooker in sink and running cold water over it.

Serve as is or over cooked rice or other grain if desired. Garnish with Parmesan cheese if desired.

Makes 8 servings

Per Serving:
186 Calories; 5g Protein; 2g Fat;
36g Carbohydrates; 0 Cholesterol;
176mg Sodium; 6g Fiber.

Tuscan Bean Stew

Serve this flavorful stew with crusty Italian rolls and a spinach salad.

1½ tablespoons olive oil
1 medium sweet or yellow
   onion, chopped
2 cloves garlic, minced
2 cups vegetable broth
One 19-ounce can cannellini
   beans, rinsed and drained
1½ teaspoons chopped fresh
   rosemary or ½ teaspoon
   dried
½ teaspoon freshly ground
   black pepper
1 large red bell pepper and 1
   large yellow bell pepper,
   roasted (see Helpful Hint)
   and julienned, or 1 jar
   roasted red peppers,
   drained and julienned
1 tablespoon balsamic vinegar

Heat oil in a large saucepan over medium heat. Add onion and garlic, cook 5 minutes, stirring occasionally. Stir in broth; bring to a boil over high heat. Stir in beans, rosemary, and pepper. Reduce heat; simmer uncovered 10 minutes, stirring occasionally. Stir in roasted peppers and vinegar; ladle into shallow bowls.

Makes 4 servings

Helpful Hint

To roast a pepper, trim, wash, seed, and flatten pepper onto a baking sheet or piece of aluminum foil. Place under broiler until pepper is completely charred. Place blackened pepper in a plastic or paper bag, seal and let steam for 10 minutes. Remove from bag. Peel charred skin with fingers.

Per Serving:
246 Calories; 11g Protein; 6g Fat;
39g Carbohydrates; 0 Cholesterol;
43mg Sodium; 8g Fiber.

Tofu Brunswick Stew

2 teaspoons canola oil
**1 pound firm tofu, drained and
    diced**
½ cup finely chopped onion
½ cup finely chopped celery
1 clove garlic, minced
1 tablespoon tomato paste
**¼ cup dry red wine or beer
    (optional)**
1 cup canned tomato puree
**¼ cup fresh or frozen (thawed)
    corn kernels**
2 tablespoons barbecue sauce
**1 tablespoon tamari (see Help-
    ful Hint) or soy sauce**
Hot pepper sauce to taste

Heat 1 teaspoon oil in a nonstick
pan over medium heat. Add tofu
and cook until browned. Remove
from pan; set aside.

Add remaining 1 teaspoon oil
to pan; add onion, celery, and
garlic and cook, stirring, until
well browned. Stir in remaining
ingredients and reserved tofu;
simmer until sauce is reduced and
develops a rich brown color, about
15 minutes.

Makes 4 servings

Helpful Hint

*Tamari is a type of Japanese soy
sauce with a dark color and rich
flavor and is usually wheat-free. It
is available in supermarkets,
natural food stores, and Asian
groceries. Regular soy sauce can be
substituted measure for measure.*

Per Serving:
154 Calories; 10g Protein; 6g Fat;
19g Carbohydrates; 0 Cholesterol;
838mg Sodium; 4g Fiber.

Spicy Red Kidney Bean Stew

*This curry-flavored stew makes a great main dish for an
Indian-inspired meal.*

3½ cups cooked red kidney
    beans (or two 15½-ounce
    cans red kidney beans)
1 cup bean cooking liquid, or
    liquid from cans plus water
    to make 1 cup
2 tablespoons canola oil
2 small onions, finely chopped
3 cloves garlic, minced
1 teaspoon curry powder
1 tomato, chopped
2 medium potatoes, cooked and
    cubed
2 carrots, cut in ½-inch cubes
    and steamed (about 1 cup)
1 tablespoon chopped fresh
    parsley

In a blender, puree 1 cup beans
with 1 cup bean liquid until
smooth, set aside. Place remaining
2½ cups beans in a separate bowl.

In a large saucepan, heat oil;
add onions and garlic and cook,
stirring, until onions are translucent, about 3 minutes. Add curry
powder and mix well. Add tomato
and reserved bean puree. Simmer,
covered, until tomato almost
dissolves in the sauce, about 10
minutes. Add potatoes and carrots
and simmer 5 minutes. Add
reserved beans and simmer
another 5 minutes. Sprinkle with
parsley and serve.

Makes 6 servings

Per Serving:
236 Calories; 10g Protein; 5g Fat;
39g Carbohydrates; 0 Cholesterol;
522mg Sodium; 12g Fiber.

Fruit Gazpacho

One 28-ounce can whole
   tomatoes, undrained
2½ cups orange juice
2 cups chopped honeydew
   melon
1 cup chopped cantaloupe
2 tablespoons raspberry vinegar
1 tablespoon brown sugar
1 teaspoon grated lime peel
½ teaspoon ground cardamom
1 cup halved, seedless red
   grapes
2 medium kiwifruit, peeled and
   chopped
½ cup fresh raspberries
Hot pepper sauce to taste

Puree tomatoes and juice in a
blender or food processor.

In a large mixing bowl, combine the tomato puree, orange
juice, melons, vinegar, sugar, lime
peel, and cardamom. Process half
of the mixture in a blender or
food processor until smooth and
return to fruit mixture. Stir in
remaining ingredients.

Makes 6 to 8 servings

Per Serving:
148 Calories; 3g Protein; 1g Fat;
35g Carbohydrates; 0 Cholesterol;
29mg Sodium; 4g Fiber.

Mushroom Chowder

2 tablespoons butter
**8 ounces fresh mushrooms,
    sliced (about 3 cups)**
¼ cup chopped onion
1 to 2 cloves garlic, minced
**2 cups diced potatoes,
    unpeeled**
1 cup water
½ cup chopped carrot
**One 10-ounce package frozen
    cream-style corn**
1 cup skim milk
**¼ teaspoon freshly ground
    black pepper**

Melt butter in a 3-quart saucepan over medium heat. Add mushrooms, onion, and garlic. Cook, stirring occasionally, until mushrooms are tender, about 5 minutes.

Stir in potatoes, water, and carrot. Cover and bring to a boil over medium-high heat; reduce heat to low. Simmer until potatoes are tender, about 10 minutes.

Add corn, milk, and pepper. Increase heat to medium-high. Cook until chowder is hot, stirring occasionally, about 5 minutes.

Makes 4 servings

Per Serving:
195 Calories; 6g Protein; 7g Fat; 32g Carbohydrates; 16mg Cholesterol; 311mg Sodium; 3g Fiber.

Cajun Beans and Pasta

Butter beans give this dish creaminess and body without fat. It's on the table in twenty-three minutes.

1½ cups (about 6 ounces) uncooked whole wheat macaroni
¼ cup vegetable broth or water
1 medium zucchini, cut in half lengthwise and sliced
½ cup finely chopped onion
One 15½-ounce can butter beans, rinsed and drained
1 medium tomato, seeded and chopped
1 to 2 teaspoons Cajun seasoning (see Helpful Hint)

Prepare the macaroni according to package directions.

While macaroni is cooking, heat the broth in a medium nonstick skillet over medium heat. Add the zucchini and onion; cook, stirring, until tender-crisp, about 5 minutes.

Stir in the beans, tomato, and Cajun seasoning. Cook until hot, stirring occasionally, about 4 minutes. Drain the pasta. Serve vegetable mixture over pasta or toss it with the pasta.

Makes 4 servings

VARIATION

Drizzle a small amount of garlic-flavored oil over individual servings.

Helpful Hint

Cajun seasoning is available in the spice aisle of most supermarkets.

Per Serving:
281 Calories; 14g Protein; 1g Fat; 58g Carbohydrates; 0 Cholesterol; 384mg Sodium; 12g Fiber.

Texas Red Chili

Traditional Texas chili is made with beef that is shredded, not ground; beans are taboo. Here, vegetable burgers replace the meat, and beans are optional, but the richly flavored sauce in this chili is absolutely authentic.

One 12.8-ounce package frozen vegetarian burgers (see Helpful Hint)
1 medium onion, chopped (about 1 cup)
1¼ cups water
One 28-ounce can diced peeled tomatoes, undrained
One 15½-ounce can dark red kidney beans, rinsed and drained (optional)
One 8-ounce can tomato sauce
One 4-ounce can minced green chile peppers
2 tablespoons tomato paste
1 tablespoon diced canned or fresh jalapeño peppers (optional)
1 tablespoon chili powder
2 teaspoons brown sugar
2 teaspoons unsweetened cocoa
1½ teaspoons dried oregano leaves
1½ teaspoons ground cumin
½ teaspoon ground cinnamon
Sour cream, plain yogurt, shredded cheese, and scallions for garnish (optional)

In a medium nonstick skillet, brown the burgers according to package directions, breaking them up with a wooden spoon as they cook.

In a 4-quart saucepan, cook the onion in ¼ cup water, stirring, over medium heat until tender, about 5 minutes; add more water as necessary to prevent sticking.

Add burgers, 1 cup water, and the remaining ingredients to the saucepan with the onion. Bring to a boil over high heat. Reduce heat to medium-low. Simmer for 10 minutes to blend flavors. Garnish as desired with sour cream, yogurt, cheese, and scallions.

Makes 6 servings

Helpful Hint

Vegetarian burgers are available in a variety of flavors and brands. Most can be found in the frozen food section of the natural food store and most supermarkets.

Per Serving:
222 Calories; 8g Protein; 8g Fat; 33g Carbohydrates; 0 Cholesterol; 835mg Sodium; 9g Fiber.

Curried Tempeh with Saffron Rice

1 cup uncooked basmati rice
    (see Helpful Hints)
Pinch saffron
1¼ cups vegetable broth or
    water
One 8-ounce package five-grain
    or plain tempeh, cut into
    1½x½-inch strips (see
    Helpful Hints)
1 medium onion, chopped
1 medium green or red bell
    pepper, seeded and
    coarsely chopped
½ cup raisins
1 tablespoon honey
2 teaspoons curry powder
½ teaspoon ground ginger
½ teaspoon ground cinnamon
¼ teaspoon ground cloves
Prepared chutney (optional; see
    Helpful Hints)

Cook the rice according to package directions, adding saffron to the cooking water.

Meanwhile, heat ¼ cup broth or water to bubbling in a large nonstick skillet over medium heat. Add tempeh, onion, and bell pepper. Cook, stirring, until vegetables are tender-crisp, about 7 minutes, adding more broth or water as necessary to prevent sticking.

Stir in remaining broth or water and the other ingredients (except chutney). Bring to a simmer and cook, stirring occasionally, until flavors are blended and sauce has thickened, about 5 minutes. Serve over hot rice with chutney on the side if desired.

Makes 4 servings

Per Serving:
353 Calories; 11g Protein; 2g Fat;
73g Carbohydrates; 0 Cholesterol;
46mg Sodium; 5g Fiber.

Helpful Hints

Basmati rice is a variety of fragrant rice that is grown in Asia and in some parts of the United States. Its flavor is perfect for Asian dishes. Basmati rice is available in natural food stores, Asian groceries, and in most supermarkets.

Chutney is a spicy East Indian condiment made from fruit, vinegar, sugar, and spices. It is a common accompaniment to curry dishes. It is sold in Indian markets and in some supermarkets.

Tempeh is a high-protein soy food with a rich taste and meaty texture that is often used as a meat substitute. It is a cake of fermented whole soybeans, usually sold in 8-ounce packages in natural food stores and in some supermarkets. Tempeh is available plain, flavored, and in combination with other grains.

Grilled Portobello Pita Pizza with Chili Aïoli

Aïoli is a flavorful garlic mayonnaise from Provence, France. In this recipe, chili powder gives it a spicy depth, making it a perfect complement to earthy portobello mushrooms.

CHILI AÏOLI:

⅓ **cup nonfat or reduced-fat mayonnaise**
1 **to 2 cloves garlic, minced**
1 **teaspoon chili powder**

PIZZA:

2 **cups lightly packed fresh assorted baby greens**
1 **tablespoon nonfat red wine vinaigrette**
4 **large fresh portobello mushrooms (about 3 ounces each), stems removed**
4 **soft pita breads or individual prepared pizza crusts**

Preheat grill or broiler.

In a small mixing bowl, combine chili aïoli ingredients; set aside.

For the pizza, in a second small mixing bowl, combine greens and vinaigrette. Toss to coat; set aside.

Grill or broil mushroom caps until nearly tender, about 6 minutes, turning once. Slice mushrooms crosswise into strips.

While mushrooms are cooking, place pita breads or pizza crusts on grill or under broiler, and cook until hot and lightly browned, about 3 minutes. Spread aïoli evenly over bread. Top with mushrooms and greens. Serve immediately.

Makes 4 servings

Per Serving:
211 Calories; 8g Protein; 1g Fat;
43g Carbohydrates; 0 Cholesterol;
585mg Sodium; 3g Fiber.

Polenta with Caramelized Onions

Polenta is Italian cornmeal mush that's a tasty base for hundreds of toppings. In this dish, it is topped with sweet, caramelized onions for an old-world comfort food.

4¼ cups water
½ teaspoon salt
1 cup coarse yellow cornmeal
1 teaspoon olive oil
2 large onions, sliced and
　　separated into rings
8 ounces fresh mushrooms,
　　sliced (about 3 cups)
3 to 4 cloves garlic, minced
2 tablespoons balsamic vinegar
Chopped fresh parsley for
　　garnish

In a 2-quart saucepan, bring 4 cups water and salt to a boil over high heat. Gradually add cornmeal, whisking to prevent lumps. Reduce heat to medium-low. Cook until thickened, whisking occasionally, about 10 minutes. Set aside and keep warm.

In a medium nonstick skillet, heat oil over medium heat. Add onions and remaining ¼ cup water. Cook, stirring, until onions become very tender, about 10 minutes. Stir in mushrooms and garlic. Continue cooking until onions and mushrooms begin to brown.

Stir vinegar into onion mixture. To serve, spoon polenta onto plates and top with the onion mixture. Garnish each serving with parsley.

Makes 4 servings

Per Serving:
167 calories; 5g protein; 3g fat; 34g Carbohydratess; 0 cholesterol; 282mg sodium; 4g fiber.

Southern Vegetable Medley

1 cup uncooked quick-cooking brown rice

One 10-ounce package frozen cut okra

1 tablespoon canola oil

1 small onion, chopped (about ½ cup)

1 stalk celery, sliced (about ½ cup)

1 to 2 cloves garlic, minced

1 teaspoon dried thyme

½ teaspoon dry mustard

¼ teaspoon freshly ground black pepper

¼ teaspoon paprika

⅛ to ¼ teaspoon cayenne pepper

One 15½-ounce can black-eyed peas, rinsed and drained

One 10-ounce package frozen corn kernels

1 to 2 medium tomatoes, chopped (1 to 2 cups)

Prepare the rice and okra according to the package directions; drain okra and set aside.

Heat oil in a medium nonstick skillet over medium-high heat. Stir in onion, celery, and garlic; cook until tender, stirring about 5 minutes. Stir in thyme, mustard, pepper, paprika, and cayenne pepper.

Add black-eyed peas and corn to skillet, stirring to combine. Cook until corn is hot and tender, stirring occasionally, about 4 minutes. Stir in okra and tomatoes. Cook until heated through, about 3 minutes. Serve over rice.

Makes 4 servings

Per Serving:
371 Calories; 12g Protein; 5g Fat;
73g Carbohydrates; 0 Cholesterol;
338mg Sodium; 10g Fiber.

Veggie Burger Stroganoff

Use your favorite kind of mushrooms in this hearty dish; mixing two or more varieties adds interest and flavor.

16 ounces uncooked fettuccine or egg noodles
One 10-ounce package nonfat or other vegetarian burgers (see Helpful Hint)
2 cups vegetable broth or water
16 ounces fresh mushrooms, sliced (about 6 cups)
1 large onion, sliced (about 1⅓ cups)
1 cup low-fat sour cream
3 tablespoons unbleached white flour
¼ teaspoon freshly ground black pepper

VARIATION

Serve stroganoff over mashed potatoes instead of fettuccine or egg noodles.

Helpful Hint

Vegetarian burgers are available in a variety of flavors and brands. Most can be found in the frozen food section of natural food stores and most supermarkets.

Prepare the fettuccine or noodles according to package directions. Drain and keep warm.

Meanwhile, brown burgers in a large nonstick skillet according to package directions. Remove burgers from skillet and cut into small pieces; set aside.

Heat ¼ cup of the broth or water in the same skillet over medium heat. Add mushrooms and onion; cook, stirring, until tender, about 6 minutes. Add remaining 1¾ cups broth or water to skillet. In a small bowl, combine sour cream, flour, and pepper; stir until smooth.

Push mushrooms and onion to one side of skillet. Gradually whisk sour cream mixture into liquid in skillet. Continue stirring until mixture comes to a boil.

Stir in burger pieces; mix well. Cook until heated through, about 3 minutes. Do not boil. Serve stroganoff over fettuccine or noodles.

Makes 8 servings

Per Serving:
318 Calories; 15g Protein; 5g Fat; 53g Carbohydrates; 95mg Cholesterol; 179mg Sodium; 4g Fiber.

Tofu Spring Rolls

Spring rolls are a more delicate version of an egg roll. They are generally wrapped with rice paper and are traditionally served on the first day of spring in the Chinese New Year, hence their name.

1 teaspoon hot chili oil (see Helpful Hints)
8 ounces firm tofu, crumbled
¾ cup sliced fresh mushrooms
½ cup mung bean sprouts
½ cup shredded carrot
2 tablespoons sliced scallions
1 tablespoon soy sauce or tamari (see Helpful Hints)
1 tablespoon rice vinegar (see Helpful Hints)
¼ teaspoon red pepper flakes
⅛ teaspoon five-spice powder (see Helpful Hints)
8 round rice-paper sheets (8½-inch diameter; see Helpful Hints) or regular egg roll wrappers
Prepared plum sauce (see Helpful Hints)

In a large nonstick skillet or a wok, heat oil over medium heat. Cook tofu, mushrooms, bean sprouts, carrot, and scallions, stirring, until sprouts are tender, about 4 minutes.

Stir in soy sauce or tamari, vinegar, red pepper flakes, and five-spice powder. Reduce heat to low; simmer for 3 minutes. Remove from heat.

Wet both sides of each rice-paper sheet by holding it briefly under cold running water. Place wet sheets on a flat surface and cover with wet paper towels. (You do not need to dampen regular egg roll wrappers.)

Place a rounded tablespoon of the tofu mixture just below the center of first rice-paper sheet. Roll up like an egg roll, folding in sides to enclose. Repeat with remaining sheets and tofu mixture.

Serve spring rolls with plum sauce for dipping.

Makes 8 spring rolls; 4 servings

Per Serving:
156 Calories; 5g Protein; 3g Fat; 28g Carbohydrates; 0 Cholesterol; 266mg Sodium; 2g Fiber.

Helpful Hints

Hot chili oil is vegetable oil infused with hot chile peppers. It is sold in Asian markets, natural food stores, and in the oil or Asian food section of supermarkets.

Tamari is a type of Japanese soy sauce with a dark color and rich flavor and is usually wheat-free. It is available in supermarkets, natural food stores, and Asian groceries. Regular soy sauce can be substituted measure for measure.

Rice vinegar is a mild vinegar made from rice that is a popular seasoning in Asian cuisines. It is excellent in sauces and salads. Rice vinegar is available in Asian markets and in most supermarkets.

Chinese five-spice powder is a mixture of equal parts of cinnamon, cloves, fennel seed, star anise, and Szechuan peppercorns. It is sold in some supermarkets and in Chinese groceries, and is easily made at home.

Rice paper is an edible, translucent, and flavorless paper made from a mixture of water and the pith of an Asian shrub called the rice-paper plant. It is used to wrap foods, and can be eaten deep-fried or as is.

Plum sauce is a condiment used in Chinese cuisine made from plums, apricots, sugar, and seasonings. Also called duck sauce, plum sauce is sold in jars in Asian markets and in the Chinese food section of supermarkets.

Sesame Eggplant and Spinach

NOODLES:

1 medium eggplant (about 20 ounces), cut crosswise into ½-inch slices

2 tablespoons sesame oil

1 tablespoon sesame seeds

One 10-ounce package frozen whole-leaf spinach

One 5-ounce package Japanese curly noodles (see Helpful Hints)

DRESSING:

3 tablespoons rice wine vinegar (see Helpful Hints)

2 teaspoons soy sauce

1 teaspoon grated fresh ginger root

½ teaspoon packed brown sugar

Preheat broiler.

For the noodles, brush both sides of eggplant slices evenly with oil. Sprinkle both sides evenly with sesame seeds. Arrange eggplant on baking sheet. Broil 5 inches from heat until eggplant is tender and browned, about 15 minutes, turning once.

Meanwhile, cook spinach and noodles according to their package directions. Drain spinach well, pressing with back of spoon to release excess liquid. Rinse noodles with hot water and drain.

In a small bowl, combine dressing ingredients; set aside.

To serve, place noodles on plates. Arrange eggplant over noodles and top with spinach. Drizzle with the dressing.

Makes 3 to 4 servings

Per Serving:
296 Calories; 12g Protein; 10g Fat; 42g Carbohydrates; 0 Cholesterol; 385mg Sodium; 9g Fiber.

Helpful Hints

Japanese curly noodles, also called chuka soba, are available in the soup or noodle aisle of most supermarkets. Ramen noodles can be substituted (save the seasoning packet for another use); however, many ramen noodles are fried and are high in fat. Be sure to purchase the baked variety.

Rice vinegar is a mild vinegar made from rice that is a popular seasoning in Asian cuisines. It is excellent in sauces and salads. Rice vinegar is available in Asian markets and in most supermarkets.

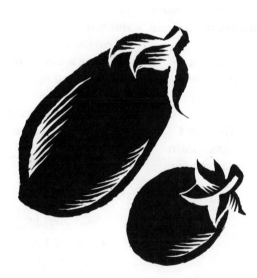

Spicy Pumpkin Burritos

Six large flour or whole wheat tortillas
1 tablespoon garlic-flavored oil (see Helpful Hints)
1 cup chopped zucchini
½ cup frozen corn kernels
¼ cup chopped onion
2 tablespoons chopped roasted jalapeño peppers (see Helpful Hints)
One 15-ounce can solid pack pumpkin
One 15½-ounce can navy beans, rinsed and drained
¼ cup water
1 teaspoon ground cumin
½ teaspoon chili powder
½ teaspoon dried oregano leaves
Shredded lettuce, chopped tomato, and nonfat plain yogurt or sour cream for toppings

Preheat oven to 200°F. Wrap tortillas in aluminum foil and place in oven to warm while preparing filling.

While tortillas are warming, heat oil in large skillet over medium heat. Add zucchini, corn, onion, and peppers; cook, stirring, until vegetables are tender-crisp, about 4 minutes.

Stir in remaining ingredients (except tortillas and toppings). Cook, stirring occasionally, until heated through, about 4 minutes.

Spoon about ½ cup pumpkin mixture across center of one tortilla. Roll up tortilla, folding in sides to enclose filling. Repeat with remaining pumpkin mixture and tortillas. Serve with toppings.

Makes 6 burritos; 6 servings

Helpful Hints

Garlic and other flavored oils are available in natural food stores, supermarkets, and gourmet food stores.

Jarred roasted jalapeño peppers are available in supermarkets.

Per Serving:
274 Calories; 11g Protein; 7g Fat; 45g Carbohydrates; 0 Cholesterol; 579mg Sodium; 8g Fiber.

Vegetable Fried Rice

Fried rice is the perfect solution to leftover rice.

1 teaspoon canola oil
¼ cup sliced scallions
1 to 2 cloves garlic, minced
2 cups sliced fresh mushrooms
1 cup halved snow pea pods
2 cups mung bean sprouts
2 cups cooked brown rice
    (½ cup raw rice)
¼ teaspoon salt
2 eggs, beaten

Heat oil in a large nonstick skillet or wok over medium-high heat. Add scallions and garlic. Cook, stirring scallions until tender, about 3 minutes. Stir in mushrooms and pea pods. Cook, stirring, until mushrooms are tender, about 5 minutes.

Add sprouts, rice, and salt until well mixed. Stir in eggs. Cook, stirring constantly, until mixture looks dry and eggs are cooked, about 4 minutes.

Makes 4 servings

Per Serving:
199 Calories; 9g Protein; 5g Fat; 31g Carbohydrates; 106mg Cholesterol; 177mg Sodium; 4g Fiber.

Tofu Chow Mein

MARINADE:

½ cup water
¼ cup soy sauce
1 tablespoon dry sherry
2 teaspoons brown sugar
2 teaspoons grated fresh ginger
    root

CHOW MEIN:

One 16-ounce package firm
    tofu, cut into ½-inch cubes
1 tablespoon canola or sesame
    oil
2 cups sliced fresh mushrooms
1 cup diagonally sliced celery
½ cup chopped red bell pepper
3 to 4 cloves garlic, minced
3 cups mung bean sprouts
One 8-ounce can bamboo
    shoots, drained (optional)
One 8-ounce can sliced water
    chestnuts, rinsed and
    drained
⅓ cup sliced scallions
3 tablespoons cornstarch
Chow mein noodles or other
    noodles, or hot cooked rice

In a shallow dish, combine marinade ingredients. Add tofu, stirring to coat. Let stand at room temperature for 10 to 15 minutes, stirring occasionally. (Prepare vegetables while tofu is marinating.)

Heat oil in a large skillet or wok over medium-high heat. Remove tofu from marinade using slotted spoon, and add it to the skillet; reserve marinade. Cook tofu in oil until it begins to brown, about 5 minutes. Stir in mushrooms, celery, bell pepper, and garlic. Cook, stirring, until celery is tender-crisp, about 5 minutes. Stir in sprouts, bamboo shoots if desired, water chestnuts, and scallions. Cook, stirring, for 2 minutes.

Stir cornstarch into reserved marinade until smooth; add to skillet. Cook, stirring constantly, until sauce thickens and becomes translucent. Serve over noodles or hot cooked rice.

Makes 6 servings

Per Serving:
138 Calories; 8g Protein; 4g Fat;
19g Carbohydrates; 0 Cholesterol;
696mg Sodium; 4g Fiber.

Greek Bulgur and Spinach Skillet Meal

2½ cups boiling water or vegetable broth
1 cup uncooked bulgur wheat
One 10-ounce package frozen chopped spinach
1 tablespoon olive oil
1 medium onion, chopped
2 cloves garlic, minced
1 teaspoon dried oregano
1 teaspoon grated lemon peel
¼ teaspoon ground nutmeg
Salt and freshly ground black pepper to taste
3 ounces feta cheese, crumbled (about ¾ cup)
2 medium tomatoes, cut into wedges

In a small mixing bowl, combine boiling water and bulgur. Set aside for 20 minutes. Meanwhile, prepare the spinach according to package directions. Drain well.

Heat oil in a medium nonstick skillet over medium heat. Add onion and garlic. Cook, stirring, until onion is tender, about 5 minutes. Stir in spinach, oregano, lemon peel, nutmeg, salt, and pepper.

Drain bulgur and fluff it with a fork. Stir bulgur into spinach mixture; mix well. Stir in feta. Garnish with tomato wedges.

Makes 4 servings

Per Serving:
242 Calories; 10g Protein; 9g Fat; 35g Carbohydrates; 19mg Cholesterol; 307mg Sodium; 9g Fiber.

Seitan Skillet Meal

*This easy, one-dish meal is a good way to use leftover wild and brown rice.
It features seitan, a meaty food made from whole wheat flour.*

1¾ cups vegetable broth or
    water
¼ cup unbleached white flour
1 teaspoon each: dried oregano,
    basil, and thyme
½ teaspoon dried marjoram
    leaves
¼ teaspoon freshly ground
    black pepper
2 teaspoons olive oil
2 medium carrots, chopped
    (about 1 cup)
1 medium onion, chopped
    (about 1 cup)
1 cup sliced fresh mushrooms
1 stalk celery, sliced (about ½
    cup)
8 ounces seitan, ground (about
    2 cups; see Helpful Hint)
1 cup cooked wild rice (about ¼
    cup raw rice)
1 cup cooked long-grain brown
    rice (about ¼ cup raw rice)
1 tablespoon chopped fresh
    parsley

In a 2-cup measure or small bowl, combine broth or water, flour, oregano, basil, thyme, marjoram, and pepper. Set aside.

In a large skillet, heat oil over medium heat. Add carrots, onion, mushrooms, and celery, and cook, stirring, until vegetables are tender-crisp, about 5 minutes.

Stir in broth mixture. Cook until sauce thickens and bubbles, stirring constantly, about 2 minutes. Stir in seitan and rices. Cook until heated through, stirring frequently. Stir in parsley.

Makes 4 to 6 servings

Helpful Hint

Seitan, also sometimes called gluten or "wheat meat," is a chewy, meatlike food made from wheat gluten and water. The gluten dough is simmered in a flavored broth, then sliced, chunked, or ground, depending on how it will be used. Its chewy texture makes it a perfect meat substitute. It can be made from whole wheat flour or from a mix found in natural food stores. It can also be purchased ready-made in natural food stores and in some Chinese markets.

Per Serving:
243 Calories, 15g Protein; 4g Fat;
45g Carbohydrates; 0 Cholesterol;
422mg Sodium; 4g Fiber.

Savory Vegetable Stir-Fry

1½ teaspoons arrowroot or
    cornstarch
1½ teaspoons cold water
¼ cup low-sodium soy sauce
¼ cup dry sherry or hot sherry
    (see Helpful Hints)
2 tablespoons toasted sesame
    oil (see Helpful Hints)
4 teaspoons regular sesame oil
4 cloves garlic, minced
4 teaspoons finely grated fresh
    ginger root
2 medium onions, thinly sliced
3 cups small cauliflower florets
⅔ cup sliced turnip
⅔ cup sliced carrot
⅔ cup sliced broccoli stems
3 cups finely chopped cabbage
3 cups small broccoli florets
8 ounces mushrooms, sliced
    (about 3 cups)
⅔ cup vegetable broth or water
6 cups cooked rice (about 1¼
    cups raw rice)

Combine arrowroot or cornstarch and cold water; stir until smooth. Set aside. In a separate bowl, whisk together soy sauce, sherry, and toasted sesame oil; set aside.

Heat a wok or large skillet. Add regular sesame oil and swirl to coat side of pan. Add garlic and ginger and stir-fry about 15 seconds. Add onions and stir-fry about 1 minute. Add remaining vegetables in order listed, a handful at a time, stir-frying about 30 seconds between each addition to maintain high heat.

Add soy sauce mixture and broth or water. Cover pan and let steam until vegetables are just tender, about 4 or 5 minutes.

Push vegetables up the side of the wok or to the sides of the pan, add arrowroot or cornstarch mixture, and stir constantly until liquid thickens. Mix vegetables back into sauce, remove from heat, and serve over rice.

Makes 4 to 6 servings

Helpful Hint

To make hot sherry, add about 12 fresh serrano peppers to a bottle of dry sherry; let steep for two weeks, then strain and use.

Dark or toasted sesame oil is more flavorful than the light or regular variety. Sesame oil is available in supermarkets, natural food stores, gourmet shops, and Asian markets.

Per Serving:
562 Calories; 13g Protein; 7g Fat;
103g Carbohydrates; 0 Cholesterol;
698mg Sodium; 12g Fiber.

Vegetable Chop Suey

⅔ cup chopped onion

3 cloves garlic, minced

2 teaspoons grated fresh
ginger root

1 tablespoon toasted or regular
sesame oil (see Helpful
Hints)

½ cup diagonally sliced carrot

½ cup diagonally sliced celery

2 cups diagonally sliced zucchini

1 cup sliced green bell peppers

⅔ cup coarsely shredded red
cabbage

⅔ cup sliced mushrooms

1 cup chopped tomatoes

⅔ cup mung bean sprouts

⅔ cup sliced green beans, cut
into 2-inch lengths

⅔ cup snow pea pods

⅔ cup bamboo shoots

⅔ cup sliced water chestnuts

1 cup water

2 tablespoons soy sauce

2 tablespoons cornstarch or
arrowroot (see Helpful
Hints)

3 cups hot cooked quick-
cooking brown rice or other
cooked rice (about ¾ cup
raw rice)

In a wok or large skillet, cook the onion, garlic, and ginger root in oil, stirring, over medium-high heat, until onion is tender-crisp. Add carrot and celery and cook, stirring, 3 minutes. Add zucchini, bell peppers, cabbage, and mushrooms, and cook 3 minutes longer.

Add tomatoes, bean sprouts, green beans, pea pods, bamboo shoots, and water chestnuts, and cook, stirring, 3 minutes.

In a small bowl, combine water, soy sauce, and cornstarch or arrowroot. Pour into vegetable mixture. Cook, stirring constantly, until the sauce is thickened and all vegetables are tender-crisp. Serve over rice.

Makes 6 servings

Helpful Hints

Dark or toasted sesame oil is more flavorful than the light or regular variety. Sesame oil is available in supermarkets, natural food stores, gourmet shops, and Asian markets.

Arrowroot is a powder derived from the arrowroot plant that is used for thickening. It is usually less processed than cornstarch and can be substituted for it measure for measure. Arrowroot is sold in natural food stores and some supermarkets.

Per Serving:
207 Calories; 5g Protein; 2g Fat;
40g Carbohydrates; 0 Cholesterol;
356mg Sodium; 6g Fiber.

Wild Rice-Orange Pancakes

Use leftover wild rice in this hearty and flavorful breakfast fare.

1 cup cooked wild rice (about ¼ cup raw rice)
¾ cup buttermilk
½ cup fresh orange juice
1 egg, lightly beaten
2 tablespoons honey or maple syrup
1 tablespoon canola oil
1 cup unbleached white flour
1 teaspoon baking powder
1 teaspoon baking soda
½ teaspoon ground cinnamon
¼ teaspoon ground nutmeg
¼ teaspoon salt

In a medium mixing bowl, combine rice, buttermilk, juice, egg, honey or maple syrup, and oil. In a small mixing bowl, combine remaining ingredients. Add dry mixture to wet ingredients, stirring until just moist.

Heat a large nonstick skillet or griddle over medium heat. Spoon about ¼ cup batter onto skillet to make a 4-inch pancake. Repeat with remaining batter. (You will have to make pancakes in batches.)

Cook until bubbles on surface of pancakes begin to subside and bottoms are golden brown, about 1 to 2 minutes. Turn pancakes and cook until bottoms are golden brown, 1 or 2 minutes more.

Makes about sixteen 4-inch pancakes; 8 servings

Per Serving:
128 Calories; 4g Protein; 2g Fat; 22g Carbohydrates; 28mg Cholesterol; 318mg Sodium; 2g Fiber.

Individual Mustard-Chèvre Pizzas

Tired of the same old pizza? Here's a twist: Dijon mustard instead of tomato sauce.

1 tablespoon Dijon mustard, or to taste

4 prepared personal-size pizza crusts

4 plum tomatoes, sliced lengthwise

3 to 4 cloves garlic, thinly sliced

4 tablespoons chèvre (goat cheese), crumbled

Preheat oven to 400°F.
Spread mustard evenly over pizza crusts. Top with tomato slices, garlic, and chèvre. Bake until crusts are browned and cheese begins to melt, about 10 minutes. Serve immediately.

Makes 4 individual-size pizzas; 4 servings

Per Pizza:
385 Calories; 16g Protein; 10g Fat; 56g Carbohydrates; 18mg Cholesterol; 981mg Sodium; 3g Fiber.

Jamaican Jerk Tempeh

4 scallions, chopped
1 small yellow onion, chopped
1 teaspoon finely chopped
 Scotch bonnet pepper or
 other chile pepper
¼ cup reduced-sodium or
 regular soy sauce
¼ cup red wine vinegar
1½ to 2 tablespoons vegetable
 oil
2 tablespoons brown sugar
1 teaspoon ground thyme
 (1 tablespoon fresh thyme
 leaves)
½ teaspoon nutmeg
½ teaspoon ground allspice
¼ teaspoon ground cloves
1 pound tempeh, cut into
 ½-inch cubes (see Helpful
 Hint)
Leaf lettuce

Preheat oven to 375°F.

Combine all ingredients except tempeh and lettuce in a blender or food processor. Process 10 to 15 seconds at high speed.

Place tempeh in a 9x13-inch casserole or baking pan and cover with sauce. Bake until tempeh is browned, 10 to 15 minutes.

To serve, remove tempeh from sauce and place on a serving plate lined with leaf lettuce. Serve remaining sauce as a dip.

Makes 4 to 6 servings

Helpful Hint

Tempeh is a high-protein soy food with a rich taste and meaty texture that is often used as a meat substitute. It is a cake of fermented whole soybeans, usually sold in 8-ounce packages in natural food stores and in some supermarkets. Tempeh is available plain, flavored, and as a combination of soybeans and other grains.

Per Serving:
255 Calories; 22g Protein; 9g Fat;
25g Carbohydrates; 0 Cholesterol;
48mg Sodium; 7g Fiber.

Lemony Light Omelet with Fresh Vegetables

3 egg whites
⅛ teaspoon cream of tartar
⅛ teaspoon white pepper
8 ounces liquid egg substitute
** or 4 eggs, beaten**
2 teaspoons toasted sesame
** seeds**
Grated peel of 1 lemon
Nonstick cooking spray
1 teaspoon sesame oil
1 cup halved broccoli florets
½ cup red bell pepper cut in
** short strips**
⅓ cup sliced onion
2 tablespoons vegetable broth
** or water**
Lemon wedges and parsley for
** garnish (optional)**

Preheat oven to 375°F.

In a medium bowl of an electric mixer, beat egg whites with cream of tartar and white pepper until soft peaks form. Fold in egg substitute or beaten eggs. Gently stir in half the sesame seeds and half the lemon peel.

Spray a medium nonstick, ovenproof skillet with nonstick cooking spray, or rub with 1 teaspoon of oil. Pour egg mixture into skillet; cook over medium heat until underside is lightly browned, about 5 minutes. Place in oven until top is set, about 6 to 7 minutes.

In a separate skillet, heat sesame oil. Add broccoli, bell pepper, onion and broth or water; sauté until vegetables are tender-crisp and liquid evaporates, about 2 to 3 minutes. Stir in remaining sesame seeds and lemon peel.

Remove omelet from oven. Loosen edges with rubber spatula. Make a cut (not quite through) across center. Slide onto large serving platter. Spoon vegetable mixture onto one half of omelet and fold other half over vegetables (mixture is puffy but will hold a folded shape if pressed lightly and held in place a few seconds). Garnish with lemon wedges and parsley if desired.

Per Serving:
99 Calories; 12g Protein; 2g Fat; 7g Carbohydrates; 0 Cholesterol; 183mg Sodium; 2g Fiber.

Makes 3 servings

Vegetable Frittata

1 tablespoon canola oil
½ cup sliced zucchini (about ½
    medium zucchini)
1 small red or green bell pepper,
    cut into ¼-inch-wide strips
1 small onion, thinly sliced
1 clove garlic, minced
½ cup chopped tomato (about
    ½ medium tomato)
½ teaspoon dried oregano
½ teaspoon dried basil
8 eggs
½ teaspoon salt
½ teaspoon freshly ground
    black pepper
½ cup shredded mozzarella
    cheese
2 tablespoons freshly grated
    Parmesan cheese (optional)

Preheat broiler.

Heat oil in ovenproof, nonstick, medium skillet over medium heat. Add zucchini, bell pepper, onion, and garlic; cook, stirring, 3 minutes. Stir in tomato, oregano, and basil. Reduce heat to medium-low.

In a medium bowl, beat eggs, salt, and pepper; stir in mozzarella cheese. Pour egg mixture over tomato mixture in skillet. Do not stir. Cover and cook until eggs are set and light brown on bottom and around edges, 9 to 11 minutes. Remove from heat and sprinkle with Parmesan cheese if desired.

Place skillet under broiler until golden brown, 2 to 3 minutes. Slice into wedges and serve.

Makes 8 servings

Per Serving:
119 Calories; 8g Protein; 8g Fat: 3g Carbohydrates; 217mg Cholesterol; 231mg Sodium; 0.7g Fiber.

Mexican Pizza

**1 thin, 12- to 14-inch homemade
or prepared pizza crust**
**One 8-ounce jar taco sauce or
picante sauce**
**One 15½-ounce can refried
beans**
1 cup shredded cheddar cheese
**¼ to ½ small head lettuce,
shredded**
2 tomatoes, chopped
**1 cup shredded taco-flavored or
Mexican-flavored cheddar
cheese**

If using homemade pizza crust,
preheat oven to 425°F. Bake crust
until light brown, about 7 minutes; cool while continuing with
recipe. Reduce oven temperature
to 375°F. If using prepared pizza
crust, preheat oven to 375°F and
proceed with recipe.

In a medium saucepan over
medium heat, combine taco or
picante sauce, and refried beans.
Mix well; cook until warm, well-
blended, and easy to spread,
about 2 minutes. Remove from
heat; spread over pizza crust.

Sprinkle cheddar cheese over
bean mixture. Bake until cheese
melts, about 2 minutes. Remove
from oven; top with lettuce,
tomatoes, and flavored cheese.
Serve immediately.

Makes 8 servings

Per Serving:
272 Calories; 13g Protein; 10g Fat;
30g Carbohydrates; 29mg Cholesterol; 763mg Sodium; 5g Fiber.

Caramelized Onion and Fresh Tomato Pizza

1 large red onion, thinly sliced
1 teaspoon olive oil
**1 tablespoon prepared basil
    pesto**
**1 large homemade or prepared
    pizza crust**
**3 medium plum tomatoes,
    sliced**
4 cloves garlic, thinly sliced
¼ cup chopped fresh basil
**⅓ cup shredded part-skim
    mozzarella cheese**
**2 tablespoons shredded freshly
    grated Parmesan cheese**

Preheat oven to 425°F.

In a medium nonstick skillet, cook the onion in oil over medium-low heat until carmelized, stirring occasionally, about 10 minutes.

Meanwhile, brush pesto evenly over pizza crust. Spread caramelized onion then tomatoes and garlic evenly over pesto. Top with remaining ingredients.

Bake the pizza until cheese is melted and crust is lightly browned, about 9 to 12 minutes.

Makes 6 servings

Per Serving:
188 Calories; 7g Protein; 2g Fat; 29g Carbohydrates; 6mg Cholesterol; 316mg Sodium; 2g Fiber.

Oriental Frittata

6 eggs
¼ cup water
1½ tablespoons soy sauce or tamari (see Helpful Hint)
¼ teaspoon freshly ground black pepper
2 tablespoons butter
1 cup halved snow pea pods
1 cup mung bean sprouts
1 medium carrot, shredded (½ cup)
¼ cup sliced scallions

In a medium mixing bowl, beat together eggs, water, soy sauce or tamari, and pepper. Set aside.

Melt butter in a medium nonstick skillet with ovenproof handle over medium heat. Add pea pods, bean sprouts, carrot, and scallions. Cook, stirring, until vegetables are tender-crisp, about 3 minutes.

Pour egg mixture over vegetables in skillet. Do not stir. Reduce heat to low, gently lifting up cooked portion with a spatula or fork so that uncooked liquid can reach the bottom of the pan. Cover and cook until almost set, about 10 to 15 minutes.

Meanwhile, preheat broiler. Place skillet under broiler with surface of egg mixture 4 inches from heat. Broil until eggs are lightly browned and no longer wet, about 4 minutes. Cut into wedges to serve.

Makes 6 servings

Helpful Hint

Tamari is a variety of Japanese soy sauce that is dark and rich tasting, and usually wheat-free. It is available in supermarkets and natural food stores. Regular soy sauce can be substituted.

If your skillet does not have an ovenproof handle, wrap the handle with heavy-duty aluminum foil before broiling frittata.

Per Serving:
133 Calories; 8g Protein; 9g Fat; 5g Carbohydrates; 222mg Cholesterol; 347mg Sodium; 1g Fiber.

Multigrain Waffles with Berry Topping

TOPPING:

1 cup sliced fresh or frozen strawberries (thawed)
¾ cup fresh or frozen blueberries (thawed)
¾ cup fresh or frozen red raspberries (thawed)
¼ cup sugar

WAFFLES:

¾ cup unbleached white flour
½ cup whole wheat flour
¼ cup oat flour
¼ cup brown rice flour
4 teaspoons baking powder
½ teaspoon salt
1½ cups buttermilk
3 eggs, separated
2 tablespoons canola oil

Preheat waffle iron.

In a medium mixing bowl, combine topping ingredients; set aside.

For the waffles, in a large mixing bowl, combine flours, baking powder, and salt; set aside. In a medium mixing bowl, combine buttermilk, egg yolks, and oil. Stir buttermilk mixture into flour mixture.

In a small mixing bowl, beat egg whites into stiff peaks. Fold egg whites into batter. Bake waffles according to manufacturer's directions for waffle iron. Serve waffles with berry topping.

Makes ten 4-inch waffles;
5 servings

Per Serving:
340 Calories; 10g Protein; 10g Fat; 52g Carbohydrates; 130mg Cholesterol; 916mg Sodium; 4g Fiber.

Baked Potato Slices and Toppings

Baked potatoes are the perfect answer when you want a quick, simple yet filling main dish. While the potatoes are baking (the microwave oven makes that chore fast), prepare the toppings to be served on top or on the side: Try steamed broccoli florets sprinkled with Parmesan or cheddar cheese, warmed leftover chili or other stew topped with sour cream or plain yogurt, cottage cheese and chives, sautéed onions and mushrooms—the options are endless.

Here's a fancier way to present baked potatoes, including a recipe for a quick, Italian-style topping.

Nonstick cooking spray
Four 8-ounce russet potatoes
**Desired toppings (recipe
    follows)**

Preheat oven to 425°F. Spray a large baking sheet with nonstick cooking spray.

Cut each potato lengthwise into ¼-inch-thick slices. Rinse slices with cold water and pat dry. Arrange slices in single layer on baking sheet. Spray slices lightly with nonstick cooking spray. Bake until potatoes are browned and tender, about 25 to 30 minutes, turning halfway through baking time.

Meanwhile, prepare a topping, such as Italian Vegetable Topping (page 129). Divide potato slices into 4 servings and fan slices out on plate. Spoon topping over potato slices.

Italian Vegetable Topping

1 tablespoon butter
1 medium zucchini, halved lengthwise and sliced (about 1⅓ cups)
1 cup sliced mushrooms
1 small onion, sliced
1 to 2 cloves garlic, minced
1 medium tomato, chopped (about 1 cup)
½ teaspoon Italian seasoning
Freshly ground black pepper to taste
Freshly grated Parmesan cheese (optional)

Melt butter in a medium skillet over medium heat. Add zucchini, mushrooms, onion, and garlic. Cook, stirring, until vegetables are tender-crisp, about 6 minutes. Stir in tomato, Italian seasoning, and pepper. Cook until heated through, about 1 minute. Spoon over potato slices. Sprinkle with Parmesan cheese if desired.

Makes 2 cups; 4 servings

**Per Serving of
Potato with Topping:**
274 Calories; 7g Protein; 3g Fat; 57g Carbohydrates; 8mg Cholesterol; 52mg Sodium; 7g Fiber.

CHAPTER 3

Side Dishes

Sautéed Zucchini and Caramelized Onions

This sweet and savory side dish also makes a great main dish when served over rice or with crusty bread.

1 to 2 tablespoons olive oil
1 medium yellow onion, sliced
    or cut into crescents
Pinch sugar
1 medium zucchini, sliced
1 large tomato, chopped
    (optional)
Pinch red pepper flakes
Salt and freshly ground black
    pepper to taste

In a large nonstick skillet, heat oil over medium-high heat. Add onion and cook, stirring, until transparent, about 5 minutes. Sprinkle with sugar; cook until onions are browned and caramelized, about 7 minutes, adding a sprinkle of water as necessary to prevent burning and sticking.

Add zucchini to skillet. Sauté until zucchini is tender, about 5 minutes. Add tomato, if desired, and red pepper flakes. Cook until heated through and tomato begins to release its juice, about 3 minutes. Add salt and pepper to taste.

Makes 4 servings

Per Serving:
50 Calories; 0.8g Protein; 4g Fat;
5g Carbohydrates; 0 Cholesterol;
2mg Sodium; 0.8g Fiber.

Braised Leeks and Mushrooms

This elegant side dish is perfect for holiday meals or any special dinner.

¼ cup dry sherry
1 teaspoon olive oil
5 cups thinly sliced leeks
    (white and green parts)
1 cup thinly sliced fresh mush-
    rooms (shiitake or chant-
    erelle), stems removed
1 tablespoon cider vinegar
1 teaspoon fresh orange juice
½ teaspoon grated orange peel
Salt and freshly ground black
    pepper to taste

In a large skillet, heat sherry and oil over medium-high heat. Add leeks. Cook leeks, stirring, for 3 minutes. Add mushrooms and cook, stirring, until mushrooms begin to weep and leeks are tender, about 5 minutes.

Stir in vinegar, orange juice, and orange peel. Remove from heat. Add salt and pepper to taste. Serve warm.

Makes 6 to 8 servings

Per Serving:
79 Calories; 1g Protein; 2g Fat;
13g Carbohydrates; 0 Cholesterol;
196mg Sodium; 3g Fiber.

Orange-Scented Asparagus

Originally formulated as a side dish for a romantic dinner for two, this citrus-flavored vegetable dish can easily be doubled to serve four.

6 ounces fresh asparagus, trimmed
½ teaspoon olive oil
1 teaspoon warm water
½ red bell pepper, seeded and julienned
1 teaspoon frozen orange juice concentrate, thawed
Freshly ground black pepper to taste
1 kiwifruit, peeled and thinly sliced
1 teaspoon brown sugar (optional)

Preheat broiler.

In a steamer or large pot of boiling water, cook asparagus until barely tender, about 7 minutes.

Meanwhile, heat oil and water in a small skillet over medium-high heat. Add bell pepper and cook, stirring, until tender-crisp, about 5 minutes. Remove from heat and gently stir in orange juice concentrate and black pepper.

Drain asparagus and arrange on two gratin dishes or other oven-proof serving dish with kiwifruit slices. Spoon bell pepper mixture over top. Sprinkle with brown sugar, if desired.

Broil until lightly browned. Serve immediately.

Makes 2 servings

VARIATION

Substitute lemon juice for orange juice and lemon slices for kiwifruit.

Per Serving:
61 Calories; 2g Protein; 1g Fat; 10g Carbohydrates; 0 Cholesterol; 6mg Sodium; 3g Fiber.

Sesame Broccoli

**2 pounds broccoli florets and
stalks, sliced into ½-inch
pieces**
1 tablespoon soy sauce
**1 tablespoon fresh lemon juice
or orange juice**
**1 teaspoon pureed or minced
fresh ginger root**
1 teaspoon sesame oil
**1 tablespoon toasted sesame
seeds (see Helpful Hint)**
**Freshly ground black pepper to
taste**

Steam broccoli until tender-crisp,
about 5 minutes. Drain; transfer to
a large serving dish.

Meanwhile, in a small bowl,
whisk together soy sauce, lemon
juice or orange juice, ginger, and
oil. Pour over broccoli and toss to
coat. Sprinkle with sesame seeds
and pepper.

Makes 6 servings

Helpful Hint

*To toast sesame seeds, place them
in a dry skillet over medium-low
heat. Cook, shaking skillet occasionally, until lightly browned.*

Per Serving:
60 Calories; 3g Protein; 2g Fat;
8g Carbohydrates; 0 Cholesterol;
209mg Sodium; 5g Fiber.

Cinnamon-Glazed Carrots

1 pound carrots, peeled and cut into ¼-inch slices
⅓ cup unsweetened apple juice concentrate, thawed
½ teaspoon ground cinnamon

Combine all ingredients in a 2-quart saucepan. Bring to a simmer over medium heat. Cover and cook until carrots are tender, 15 to 20 minutes.

Uncover and continue cooking until liquid is reduced to a glaze, about 4 minutes.

Makes 6 servings

Per Serving:
60 Calories; 1g Protein; 0.1g Fat; 14g Carbohydrates; 0 Cholesterol; 55mg Sodium; 3g Fiber.

Southern-Style Ranch Beans

Nonstick cooking spray
2 medium onions, chopped
2 tablespoons water
Three 16-ounce cans vegetarian baked beans
One 16-ounce can stewed tomatoes, undrained
One 15½-ounce can kidney beans, rinsed and drained
1 cup brown sugar
2 tablespoons prepared mustard
1 tablespoon apple cider vinegar

Spray a large nonstick skillet with nonstick cooking spray. Cook onions in water, stirring, over medium-high heat until onions are tender and water has evaporated.

Stir in remaining ingredients. Cover; simmer for 15 minutes, stirring occasionally.

Makes 10 to 12 servings

Per Serving:
345 Calories; 11g Protein; 1g Fat; 36g Carbohydrates; 0 Cholesterol; 1,127mg Sodium; 17g Fiber.

Apple-Onion Stuffed Zucchini

2 medium zucchini
2 teaspoons butter or olive oil
1 Granny Smith apple, chopped
1 small onion, chopped
⅓ to ½ cup seasoned bread
    crumbs

Preheat oven to 375°F.

Cut zucchini in half lengthwise. Make a cavity in the zucchini halves by scraping out pulp with a spoon; reserve pulp. Set zucchini aside.

Heat butter or olive oil in a medium skillet over medium-low heat. Add apple, onion, and zucchini pulp; cook, stirring, until tender, about 10 minutes. Add bread crumbs; stir to coat.

Place zucchini shells in baking pan with enough water to cover bottom of pan. Spoon apple mixture evenly into shells. Bake until browned on top, about 15 to 20 minutes. Bake longer depending on desired doneness.

Makes 4 servings

Per Serving:
94 Calories; 3g Protein; 2g Fat; 17g Carbohydrates; 5mg Cholesterol; 284mg Sodium; 3g Fiber.

Spinach with Garbanzos, Pine Nuts, and Raisins

1 tablespoon olive oil
1 large onion, chopped
1 large clove garlic, minced
One 10-ounce package frozen spinach, thawed and squeezed dry
One 15½-ounce can garbanzo beans (chickpeas), undrained
1 cup raisins
¼ to ½ cup toasted pine nuts (see Helpful Hint)
½ teaspoon ground nutmeg
Salt and freshly ground black pepper to taste
¼ cup nonfat plain yogurt (optional)

In a large skillet, heat oil over medium heat. Add onion and garlic; cook, stirring, until onion begins to soften, about 5 minutes. Transfer to blender or food processor. Add spinach; process until smooth. Return to skillet.

Add beans, raisins, pine nuts, nutmeg, salt, and pepper. Cook, stirring, for 5 minutes more. Stir in yogurt, if desired. Serve hot.

Makes 4 servings

Helpful Hint

To toast pine nuts, place them in a dry skillet over medium heat. Stir nuts or shake pan until nuts are browned. Immediately remove from pan to prevent burning.

Per Serving:
360 Calories; 12g Protein; 10g Fat; 63g Carbohydrates; 0 Cholesterol; 657mg Sodium; 10g Fiber.

Vegan Caesar Salad

If you love Caesar salad but no longer eat anchovies, here is a vegetarian version so delicious you'll never miss the fish.

3 tablespoons Dijon mustard
3 tablespoons nutritional yeast
flakes (see Helpful Hint)
2 tablespoons blanched and
ground almonds
3 cloves garlic, minced
¼ cup water
3 tablespoons fresh lemon juice
2 tablespoons soy sauce
1 tablespoon olive oil (optional)
1 large head romaine lettuce,
torn into large pieces
1½ cups prepared croutons

In a small mixing bowl, combine mustard, yeast flakes, almonds, and garlic to make a paste. Whisk in water, lemon juice, soy sauce, and olive oil if desired; set aside. Alternatively, combine all ingredients (except lettuce and croutons) in a food processor or blender and process until smooth.

In a large salad bowl, combine romaine lettuce and croutons. Add dressing and toss to coat. Serve immediately.

Makes 6 servings

Helpful Hint

Nutritional yeast is a dietary supplement that looks like yellowish-brown flakes and has a nutty, cheesy taste. It can be added to soups and stews or baked goods. It is sold in natural food stores.

Per Serving:
90 Calories; 5g Protein; 3g Fat;
11g Carbohydrates; 0 Cholesterol;
574mg Sodium; 2g Fiber.

Scored Baby Eggplant with Tomatoes, Capers, and Scallions

**4 baby eggplants, halved
  lengthwise**
**½ cup finely chopped seeded
  tomato**
½ cup finely chopped scallions
**¼ cup finely chopped fresh
  basil (2 tablespoons dried)**
**2 tablespoons chopped capers,
  rinsed and drained**
2 tablespoons tomato paste
1 teaspoon olive oil
**1 teaspoon white or green
  peppercorns, coarsely
  crushed (optional)**

Preheat oven to 400°F.

Score eggplant halves crosswise and diagonally on cut surface. Arrange cut-side up on baking sheet. Bake until tender, about 15 minutes. Remove from oven. Preheat broiler.

Meanwhile, combine remaining ingredients in medium bowl. Spoon mixture evenly over baked eggplant halves, pressing firmly with back of spoon to open the eggplants slightly.

Place eggplants under broiler with surface about 4 inches from heat. Broil until topping is just heated through, about 1 minute. Garnish with additional fresh basil if desired. Serve hot or at room temperature.

Makes 4 servings

Helpful Hint

Baked eggplants can be wrapped in aluminum foil and refrigerated up to 2 days before broiling.

Per Serving:
52 Calories; 1g Protein; 1g Fat;
9g Carbohydrates; 0 Cholesterol;
12mg Sodium; 3g Fiber.

141

Warm New Potato Salad

SALAD:

**1 pound new potatoes,
    unpeeled, cut into quarters
    (about 3 cups)**
1 to 2 cups water
**2 cups frozen mixed vegetables
    of your choice**

DRESSING:

**¼ cup nonfat or low-fat plain
    yogurt**
2 tablespoons mayonnaise
1 tablespoon Dijon mustard
**1 tablespoon finely chopped
    fresh Italian parsley or
    cilantro**
**2 teaspoons finely chopped
    fresh dill**
**Freshly ground black pepper to
    taste**

For the salad, in a 2-quart sauce-pan, combine potatoes and water. Bring to a boil over high heat. Cover; reduce heat to low. Simmer until potatoes are tender-crisp, about 10 minutes.

Stir in vegetable mixture. Cover and increase heat to medium-high. Cook until potatoes are tender and vegetables are hot, stirring occa-sionally, about 4 minutes. Drain.

For the dressing, while veg-etables are cooking, combine remaining ingredients in a serving bowl. Add potato mixture; toss gently to coat. Serve warm.

Makes 6 servings

Per Serving:
125 Calories; 3g Protein; 4g Fat;
19g Carbohydrates; 2mg Choles-terol; 118mg Sodium; 3g Fiber.

New Potatoes with Horseradish Sauce

**2 pounds small new potatoes,
    unpeeled**
**1 cup low-fat plain yogurt or
    pureed soft silken tofu**
**3-inch piece fresh horseradish
    root, peeled and grated (or
    ¼ cup bottled, grated
    horseradish)**
⅛ teaspoon sugar
Salt and white pepper to taste

Gently steam potatoes in a large covered pot with 1 inch of water until they can be pierced easily with a fork, about 20 minutes. Drain.

Combine remaining ingredients in a small bowl. Combine with potatoes in a large serving bowl; toss gently to coat. Serve warm.

Makes 4 to 6 servings

Per Serving:
244 Calories; 8g Protein; 1g Fat; 52g Carbohydrates; 4mg Cholesterol; 201mg Sodium; 4g Fiber.

Pesto Mashed Potatoes

6 medium russet potatoes
½ cup firmly packed fresh basil
1 tablespoon olive oil
1 tablespoon freshly grated
Parmesan cheese
2 small cloves garlic
2 tablespoons nonfat dried milk
powder
White pepper to taste

Peel potatoes if desired, and coarsely chop. Place potatoes in a large pot, cover potatoes with water, and bring to a boil over high heat. Reduce heat to medium; simmer until potatoes are very tender, about 15 to 20 minutes. Drain and place in a large serving bowl.

While potatoes are cooking, combine basil, oil, cheese, and garlic in a blender or food processor. Process until smooth; set aside.

With an electric mixer, whip potatoes, gradually adding milk powder, until light and fluffy. Stir pesto into potatoes. Add white pepper to taste. Serve immediately.

Makes 6 to 8 servings

Per Serving:
157 Calories; 3g Protein; 2g Fat; 30g Carbohydrates; 1mg Cholesterol; 37mg Sodium; 3g Fiber.

Mojo Potatoes

Mojo sauce is a tart and spicy mixture used in the Canary Islands. There, potatoes are cooked in seawater and topped with this sauce.

8 cups water
1 to 2 teaspoons salt
12 medium red potatoes,
    unpeeled, cut into quarters
2 tablespoons red wine vinegar
2 tablespoons olive oil
1 tablespoon water
2 teaspoons finely chopped
    fresh parsley
2 cloves garlic, minced
¾ teaspoon paprika
¾ teaspoon cumin seeds,
    toasted and slightly
    crushed (see Helpful Hint)
½ teaspoon salt or to taste
⅛ teaspoon red pepper flakes
    or to taste

In a 6-quart stockpot, combine 8 cups water and 1 to 2 teaspoons salt. Bring to a boil over high heat. Add potatoes and return to a boil. Reduce heat to medium and simmer until potatoes are tender, about 15 minutes. Drain.

While potatoes are cooking, whisk together vinegar, oil, and water in a small bowl. Whisk in remaining ingredients.

Pour sauce over drained potatoes; toss gently to coat. Serve hot or warm.

Makes 6 to 8 servings

Helpful Hint

To toast cumin seeds, place them in a dry skillet over medium-low heat. Stir seeds or shake pan frequently to prevent burning, until seeds are lightly browned.

Per Serving:
281 Calories; 4g Protein; 3g Fat;
56g Carbohydrates; 0 Cholesterol;
546mg Sodium; 5g Fiber.

Parslied Bulgur Pilaf

*Bulgur—hulled, cracked wheat—can be used for more than tabouli.
It is a hearty change from rice and pasta.*

1½ cups uncooked bulgur
2 cups boiling water or vegetable stock
1½ teaspoons olive oil
¼ cup finely chopped fresh
   parsley
½ teaspoon salt
½ teaspoon freshly ground
   black pepper

Combine bulgur and boiling water
or stock in a small bowl. Cover;
set aside for 20 minutes. Drain.

Heat oil in a medium skillet
over medium heat. Add bulgur
and cook, stirring, for 2 minutes.
Stir in parsley, salt, and pepper.
Serve hot.

Makes 2 servings

Per Serving:
485 Calories; 17g Protein; 4g Fat;
95g Carbohydrates; 0 Cholesterol;
549mg Sodium; 13g Fiber.

Indonesian Fried Rice

A spicy, curry-flavored version of fried rice, this dish is called
nasi goreng *in Indonesia.*

2 to 4 tablespoons peanut oil
2 medium onions, chopped
2 cloves garlic, minced
½ to 2 teaspoons red pepper
   flakes
2 teaspoons ground coriander
1 teaspoon ground cumin
1 to 2 cups fresh mung bean
   sprouts
4 cups cold cooked brown rice
   (about 1 cup raw rice)
2 tablespoons soy sauce mixed
   with 1 tablespoon brown
   sugar
2 eggs, scrambled or fried
   (optional)

Heat oil in a wok or large skillet over medium-high heat. Add onions, garlic, red pepper flakes, coriander, and cumin. Stir-fry until onions are tender, about 6 minutes.

Add bean sprouts and cook, stirring, for 2 minutes more. Add rice, a little at a time, stir-frying until rice is thoroughly heated, about 5 to 10 minutes.

Remove from heat. Stir in soy sauce–sugar mixture. Garnish with eggs, if desired. Serve hot.

Makes 12 servings

VARIATION

Substitute an Indonesian soy sauce called kecap manis *for the soy sauce–sugar mixture.*

Per Serving:
115 Calories; 3g Protein; 2g Fat;
20g Carbohydrates; 0 Cholesterol;
151mg Sodium; 2g Fiber.

Rice Noodles with Ginger and Snow Peas

8 ounces uncooked rice noodles
1½ to 3 tablespoons canola oil
1 tablespoon peeled and sliv-
**   ered fresh ginger root**
3 cloves garlic, minced
20 snow pea pods, trimmed
½ cup finely shredded carrots
3 scallions, thinly sliced (green
**   and white parts)**
1 fresh jalapeño pepper, seeded
**   and finely chopped**
½ teaspoon salt
Dash sesame oil (optional)
Dash hot chili oil (optional)
Chopped fresh cilantro or
**   parsley for garnish**

Prepare rice noodles according to package directions until *al dente*. Drain and set aside.

Heat oil in a large skillet over medium heat; cook ginger and garlic, stirring, for 1 minute. Add pea pods, carrots, scallions, and jalapeño pepper; cook, stirring, for 2 minutes. Stir in salt.

Add noodles, tossing to coat. Remove from heat. If desired, add sesame oil and chili oil; toss to coat. Garnish with cilantro or parsley.

Makes 3 to 4 servings

Per Serving:
213 Calories; 6g Protein; 9g Fat;
26g Carbohydrates; 0 Cholesterol;
372mg Sodium; 7g Fiber.

Sesame Noodles

This recipe is great for picnics and potlucks because its flavor improves with time and is ideally served at room temperature.

8 ounces uncooked linguine or Chinese-style noodles
3 scallions, sliced
1 tablespoon soy sauce
1 tablespoon sesame oil (see Helpful Hints)
1 tablespoon chopped fresh cilantro
2 teaspoons toasted sesame seeds (see Helpful Hints)
1 clove garlic, minced
¼ teaspoon red pepper flakes

Break linguine in half, if using. Prepare linguine or noodles according to package directions until *al dente*. Drain and transfer to large mixing bowl.

Add remaining ingredients; toss to combine. Serve hot or at room temperature.

Makes 4 servings

Helpful Hints

For a richer sesame flavor, use toasted sesame oil.

To toast sesame seeds, place them in a dry skillet over medium-low heat. Stir seeds or shake pan frequently to prevent burning, until seeds are lightly browned.

Per Serving:
208 Calories; 8g Protein; 5g Fat; 32g Carbohydrates; 93mg Cholesterol; 306mg Sodium; 2g Fiber.

Grilled Vegetable Kebabs

Nonfat salad dressings make great marinades for grilled foods. Use the honey-Dijon dressing recommended in this recipe or substitute it with your favorite dressing.

1 medium eggplant
2 medium yellow summer squash
1 red bell pepper
1 medium Anaheim pepper or green bell pepper
1 medium onion
1 cup prepared honey-Dijon dressing
Six large skewers (see Helpful Hint)

Preheat grill.

Cut eggplant in half lengthwise. Cut halves into 1-inch-thick slices. Cut each squash into ³/₄-inch slices. Remove seeds from peppers and cut them into large chunks. Cut onion into wedges.

Combine all vegetables in a shallow dish. Pour dressing over vegetables, stirring to coat. Let stand at room temperature for 10 minutes.

Thread vegetables evenly onto skewers. Place kebabs on grill; brush with dressing from dish. Grill kebabs until desired doneness, 10 to 15 minutes, turning kebabs and basting occasionally.

Makes 6 servings

Per Serving:
197 Calories; 6g Protein; 1g Fat; 33g Carbohydrates; 0 Cholesterol; 1,185mg Sodium; 6g Fiber.

VARIATIONS

For variety and freshness, use other seasonal vegetables. Make sure they are of similar crispness and density, so they cook evenly.

The kebabs become a main dish when served over hot rice or other hot grain.

For a heartier dish, add cubes of firm tofu to the kebabs.

Helpful Hints

If using wooden skewers, soak them in warm water while preparing the vegetables to prevent them from burning on the grill.

For easy cleanup, spray cooking grate with nonstick cooking spray before grilling.

Cajun Kale

1 tablespoon garlic-flavored oil
(see Helpful Hints) or olive
oil
8 ounces fresh mushrooms,
sliced (about 3 cups)
1 small onion, chopped (about
½ cup)
2 teaspoons Cajun seasoning
(see Helpful Hints)
8 cups (about 1 pound) torn
fresh kale, large stems
removed
1 medium tomato, chopped
(about 1 cup)

Heat oil in a large nonstick skillet over medium-high heat. Add mushrooms and onion; cook, stirring, until tender, about 5 minutes. Stir in Cajun seasoning. Reduce heat to medium.

Stir in kale. Cook, stirring, just until kale is tender, about 6 minutes. Stir in tomato and heat until just warm, about 1 minute.

Makes 4 servings

VARIATION

Cajun Kale easily becomes a main dish when served over hot rice or other grains.

Helpful Hints

Garlic oil and other flavored oils are sold in most supermarkets and natural food stores.

Cajun seasoning is sold in the spice aisle of most supermarkets.

Per Serving:
126 Calories; 6g Protein; 5g Fat;
19g Carbohydrates; 0 Cholesterol;
64mg Sodium; 4g Fiber.

Steamed Asparagus with Raspberry-Yogurt Sauce

1 pound trimmed fresh aspara-gus (about 20 spears)
¼ cup nonfat plain yogurt
2 tablespoons finely chopped red bell pepper
2 tablespoons raspberry vinegar
½ teaspoon sugar
⅛ teaspoon fennel seed, crushed
Salt and freshly ground black pepper to taste

Steam asparagus until bright green and just tender, about 6 minutes. (Steam longer if more tender asparagus is desired.)

Meanwhile, combine remaining ingredients in a small bowl; whisk well.

Arrange asparagus on a serving platter. Drizzle yogurt sauce over asparagus. Serve immediately.

Makes 4 servings

Per Serving:
40 Calories; 4g Protein; 0.9g Fat; 7g Carbohydrates; 0.9mg Cholesterol; 158mg Sodium; 2g Fiber.

Oven Vegetable Fries

You don't have to forgo fried potatoes when you're trying to eat low in fat; baked potatoes like these can also satisfy.

Nonstick cooking spray
4 cups (1⅓ cups each) thinly
sliced unpeeled russet
potato, peeled sweet
potato, and peeled parsnip
strips (3 x ¼-inch strips)
2 teaspoons olive oil
½ teaspoon seasoned salt
¼ teaspoon freshly ground
black pepper

Preheat oven to 400°F. Spray a large baking sheet with nonstick cooking spray. In a large bowl, combine vegetable strips and oil; toss to coat. Add seasoned salt and pepper; toss again. Arrange strips in a single layer on baking sheet.

Bake until vegetables are tender and lightly browned, about 20 minutes, stirring once or twice.

Makes 4 servings

VARIATIONS

Combine potatoes and parsnips in any proportion to equal 4 cups.

For crisper fries, bake an additional 5 to 10 minutes.

Substitute 1 to 2 teaspoons Cajun seasoning, herbed seasoning blend, or other seasoning blend for salt and pepper.

Per Serving:
154 Calories; 2g Protein; 2g Fat; 32g Carbohydrates; 0 Cholesterol; 183mg Sodium; 4g Fiber.

Roasted Eggplant with Orange-Miso Glaze

EGGPLANT:

Nonstick cooking spray
**1 medium eggplant (about 20
   ounces), cut into ½-inch
   slices**
1 tablespoon olive oil

GLAZE:

2 tablespoons orange juice
**1 tablespoon light miso (see
   Helpful Hint)**
1 tablespoon honey
½ teaspoon grated orange peel
Dash cayenne pepper

Preheat oven to 400°F. Arrange eggplant slices on baking sheet that has been sprayed with nonstick cooking spray. Brush tops of slices evenly with olive oil. Bake for 10 minutes.

Meanwhile, combine glaze ingredients in a small bowl; whisk until smooth. Turn eggplant slices over. Brush evenly with half of glaze. Bake for 5 minutes. Brush slices evenly with remaining glaze. Bake until eggplant is tender, about 5 minutes.

Makes 6 servings

Helpful Hint

Miso is a salty paste made from cooked, aged soybeans and sometimes grains. Thick and spreadable, it's used for flavoring and soup bases. Darker varieties are stronger in flavor than lighter varieties. Available in natural food stores and Japanese and Chinese markets.

Per Serving:
63 Calories; 1g Protein; 3g Fat;
10g Carbohydrates; 0 Cholesterol;
108mg Sodium; 3g Fiber.

Garlic Green Beans

**1 pound fresh green beans, left
whole or trimmed and cut
into 2- to 3-inch lengths**
1 tablespoon olive oil
**2 cloves garlic, minced, or to
taste**
**¼ cup plain or seasoned bread
crumbs**
**¼ teaspoon freshly ground
black pepper**

Steam beans until tender-crisp,
about 10 minutes. Set aside and
keep warm.

In a large, deep skillet, heat oil
over medium-low heat. Add
garlic. Cook, stirring, for 2
minutes. Do not let garlic brown.
Stir in bread crumbs and pepper.
Cook for 1 minute more.

Add beans; stir to coat. Serve
immediately.

Makes 4 to 6 servings

Helpful Hints

*To save time, heat water for
steaming while trimming beans.*

*For a different flavor, substitute an
herb-flavored oil for olive oil.*

Per Serving:
95 Calories; 3g Protein; 4g Fat;
14g Carbohydrates; 0.9mg Cholesterol; 202mg Sodium; 3g Fiber.

Green Beans with
Fresh Mozzarella and Tomato

1 pound frozen green beans
½ cup finely chopped red onion
½ cup water
1 medium tomato, seeded and
    chopped (about 1 cup)
4 ounces fresh mozzarella
    cheese, cut into small cubes
2 tablespoons finely chopped
    fresh basil (or 2 teaspoons
    dried basil)
2 tablespoons nonfat Italian
    dressing

Cook green beans, onion, and water in a 2-quart saucepan until green beans are tender; drain and return to saucepan.

While green beans and onion are cooking, prepare tomatoes and cheese.

Gently stir in tomato, cheese, and basil with drained green beans and onion. Add dressing and toss to coat. Serve warm.

Makes 6 to 8 servings

VARIATION

You can substitute fresh green beans for frozen and steam until tender, about 10 minutes.

Per Serving:
84 Calories; 6g Protein; 3g Fat; 9g Carbohydrates; 11mg Cholesterol; 148mg Sodium; 3g Fiber.

Squash Puree with Dates

**Two 12-ounce packages frozen
cooked winter squash,
thawed**
½ cup chopped dates or raisins
2 tablespoons maple syrup
⅛ to ¼ teaspoon ground nutmeg
**Salt and freshly ground black
pepper to taste**
¼ cup pecans

Preheat oven to 375°F.

In a medium bowl, combine squash, dates or raisins, maple syrup, nutmeg, salt, and pepper. Spoon mixture evenly into a 9-inch pie plate. Sprinkle nuts evenly over top.

Bake until heated through, about 15 minutes.

Makes 4 to 6 servings

Per Serving:
201 Calories; 3g Protein; 5g Fat;
39g Carbohydrates; 0 Cholesterol;
137mg Sodium; 7g Fiber.

Cucumber Raita

A raita is a cooling yogurt-based salad that is a traditional accompaniment to spicy-hot Indian dishes. Toasted coriander, cumin, and fennel seeds lend this one a unique flavor.

1 cup plain yogurt (see Helpful Hint)
2 large cucumbers, peeled and finely chopped (about 4 cups)
½ cup frozen peas, thawed
½ cup finely chopped radishes
1 fresh jalapeño pepper or other chile pepper, seeded and diced
1 to 2 teaspoons coriander seeds
1 to 2 teaspoons cumin seeds
¼ to ½ teaspoon fennel seeds
½ teaspoon salt
¼ teaspoon freshly ground black pepper

In a medium mixing bowl, whisk yogurt until smooth. Add cucumbers, peas, radishes, and jalapeño or other chile pepper; stir to combine. Set aside.

In a small dry skillet, combine coriander, cumin, and fennel seeds. Cook over medium-low heat until toasted, about 2 minutes, shaking pan frequently to prevent burning.

Coarsely crush seeds with a mortar and pestle or the flat side of a chef's knife. Stir crushed seeds, salt, and pepper into yogurt mixture. Serve raita chilled or at room temperature.

Makes 4 to 6 servings

Helpful Hint

For best results, do not use nonfat or low-fat yogurt for this recipe, because the salad will become watery. Use a rich, creamy yogurt or low-fat yogurt cheese (see page 13 for technique).

Per Serving:
97 Calories; 6g Protein; 3g Fat; 13g Carbohydrates; 13mg Cholesterol; 508mg Sodium; 3g Fiber.

Southwestern Corn

2 cups frozen corn kernels
**½ cup finely chopped green
   bell pepper**
**½ cup finely chopped red bell
   pepper**
½ cup water
¼ cup finely chopped red onion
**2 tablespoons finely chopped
   fresh cilantro (optional)**
1 tablespoon balsamic vinegar
1 teaspoon olive oil
½ teaspoon ground cumin
**Salt and freshly ground black
   pepper to taste**

In a 2-quart saucepan, combine corn, bell peppers, water, and onion. Bring to a boil over high heat. Cover. Reduce heat to medium-low. Simmer until vegetables are tender-crisp, about 6 minutes, stirring occasionally. Drain. Stir in remaining ingredients.

Makes 4 servings

Per Serving:
87 Calories; 3g Protein; 1g Fat;
19g Carbohydrates; 0 Cholesterol;
138mg Sodium; 2g Fiber.

Ginger-Glazed Carrots

Crystallized ginger gives the carrots in this understated and elegant side dish a mild, yet distinct bite.

2 cups sliced peeled carrots
¼ cup water
1 tablespoon finely chopped
   crystallized ginger
1 teaspoon butter (optional)
Salt to taste

Combine all ingredients except salt in a 2-quart saucepan. Bring to a boil over high heat. Cover and reduce heat to medium-low. Simmer until carrots are tender-crisp, about 6 minutes, stirring once.

Remove lid. Increase heat to medium. Simmer until liquid is nearly evaporated, about 4 minutes, stirring occasionally. Add salt to taste.

Makes 3 to 4 servings

Per Serving:
48 Calories; 1g Protein; 0.9g Fat; 11g Carbohydrates; 0 Cholesterol; 158mg Sodium; 3g Fiber.

Shredded Zucchini Sauté

2 teaspoons herb-flavored oil
  (see Helpful Hints)
2 medium zucchini, coarsely
  shredded
1 clove garlic, minced
¼ cup roasted red bell pepper
  in marinade, drained and
  cut into strips (see Helpful
  Hints)
1 tablespoon freshly grated
  Parmesan cheese
2 teaspoons balsamic vinegar
  (optional)
Freshly ground black pepper to
  taste

Heat oil in a large nonstick skillet over medium heat. Add zucchini and garlic. Cook, stirring, until zucchini is tender, about 5 minutes. Remove from heat.

Stir in remaining ingredients. Serve immediately.

Makes 3 to 4 servings

Helpful Hint

Herb oil and other flavored oils are sold in most supermarkets and natural food stores.

To reduce fat further, use freshly roasted red bell pepper. To roast a pepper, place it under a broiler with surface 3 to 4 inches from heat. Turn pepper frequently until skin is blackened. Seal pepper in a plastic or paper bag and let steam for 10 minutes. Peel and proceed with recipe as directed. (Pepper can also be held over a gas flame to roast with a long-handled fork.)

Per Serving:
77 Calories; 2g Protein; 7g Fat; 4g Carbohydrates; 1mg Cholesterol; 34mg Sodium; 1g Fiber.

Tabbouleh

This is the classic hearty vegetarian salad.

BULGUR:

2 cups water
1 cup uncooked medium-grain bulghur
1 medium tomato, seeded and finely chopped
1 cup finely chopped fresh parsley
¼ cup thinly sliced scallions

DRESSING:

½ cup fresh lemon juice
2 tablespoon olive oil
½ teaspoon salt
½ teaspoon freshly ground black pepper

For the bulgur, in a small saucepan, bring water to a boil over high heat. Stir in bulgur. Remove from heat. Set aside for 20 minutes.

Meanwhile, prepare tomato, parsley, and scallions.

Combine dressing ingredients in a 1-cup measure or small bowl; whisk well.

Drain bulgur; rinse well with cold water and drain again. Place bulgur in a medium mixing bowl. Stir in tomato, parsley, and scallions. Add dressing; toss to coat.

Makes 8 servings

VARIATIONS

For a light main dish or an appetizer, serve in an avocado half.

Add about 1 cup peeled and diced cucumber.

Helpful Hint

The flavor of the tabbouleh improves if it is chilled for a few hours (stir occasionally).

Per Serving:
107 Calories; 3g Protein; 4g Fat; 18g Carbohydrates; 0 Cholesterol; 156mg Sodium; 4g Fiber.

Cranberry Wild Rice

This flavorful side dish is perfect for holiday and harvest time, and is a delicious way to use up leftover cooked wild rice and brown rice. Try it as a stuffing for baked acorn squash halves.

1 cup fresh or frozen
    cranberries
½ cup brown sugar
¼ cup sliced almonds
2 cups cooked wild rice (about
    ½ cup raw rice)
1 cup cooked brown rice (about
    ¼ cup raw rice)
½ cup sliced celery
⅓ cup fresh orange juice
2 tablespoons red wine vinegar
1 teaspoon grated orange peel

In a medium nonstick skillet, cook cranberries, sugar, and almonds over medium heat, stirring constantly until sugar melts and coats cranberries and almonds, about 6 minutes.

Stir in remaining ingredients. Cook until heated through, about 5 minutes, stirring frequently.

Makes 10 servings

Per ½ Cup:
112 Calories; 3g Protein; 2g Fat;
22g Carbohydrates; 0 Cholesterol;
10mg Sodium; 2g Fiber.

Warm Fruited Couscous

2 cups water
1 cup uncooked couscous (see
    Helpful Hint)
2 medium kiwifruit, peeled and
    chopped
1 cup halved seedless red
    grapes
1 medium mango, peeled and
    chopped
½ cup fresh red raspberries
⅓ cup fresh orange juice
¼ cup honey
2 tablespoons raspberry
    vinegar
2 teaspoons grated lime peel
1½ teaspoons poppy seeds
⅛ teaspoon white pepper
Lettuce leaves

In a 2-quart saucepan, bring water to a boil over high heat. Stir in couscous. Cover and remove from the heat. Set aside for 5 minutes.

Meanwhile, in a large bowl, combine the kiwifruit, grapes, mango, and raspberries. In a 2-cup measure or small bowl, combine the remaining ingredients (except lettuce); whisk until well combined.

Fluff couscous with a fork. Add the couscous to the fruit mixture; stir gently to combine. Add orange juice mixture to couscous mixture. Stir gently to combine. Serve immediately over lettuce leaves.

Makes 4 to 6 servings

Helpful Hint

Couscous is steamed, dried, and crushed durum wheat common in Middle Eastern cuisine. It is sold in supermarkets and natural food stores. Couscous cooks up quickly and is a good alternative to rice or other grains.

Per Serving:
296 Calories; 6g Protein; 1g Fat;
70g Carbohydrates; 0 Cholesterol;
10mg Sodium; 4g Fiber.

Couscous Pilaf with Sun-Dried Tomatoes

This recipe makes enough for a crowd, but it can easily be halved.

6 cups vegetable stock
1 cup chopped onion or scallions
¼ cup slivered sun-dried tomatoes in oil, drained
2 cloves garlic, minced
2½ cups uncooked couscous (see Helpful Hint)
Dash turmeric
Salt and freshly ground black pepper to taste
Paprika for garnish (if desired)

In a 3-quart saucepan, combine stock, onion or scallions, tomatoes, and garlic. Bring to a boil over high heat.

Stir in couscous, turmeric, salt, and pepper. Cover and remove from heat. Let stand for 5 minutes. Fluff with a fork. Garnish with paprika, if desired.

Makes 8 servings

Helpful Hint

Couscous is steamed, dried, and crushed durum wheat common in Middle Eastern cuisine. It is sold in supermarkets and natural food stores. Couscous cooks up quickly and is a good alternative to rice or other grains.

Per Serving:
162 Calories; 5g Protein; 1g Fat;
35g Carbohydrates; 0 Cholesterol;
144mg Sodium; 1g Fiber.

Quinoa with Caramelized Onions

Quinoa, a fast-cooking, flavorful grain originally from South America, goes well with the rich flavor of caramelized onions in this Greek-style dish.

1½ cups uncooked quinoa, rinsed well and drained (see Helpful Hint)
1 medium onion, chopped
1 tablespoon olive oil
¼ cup vegetable broth
2 tablespoons finely chopped fresh parsley
2 tablespoons fresh lemon juice
1½ teaspoons dried oregano leaves
Salt and freshly ground black pepper to taste
1 medium tomato, seeded and chopped

Rinse quinoa well before cooking. Prepare quinoa according to package directions.

Meanwhile, combine onion and oil in a medium nonstick skillet. Cook over medium-high heat until onion is browned, about 15 minutes, stirring frequently. (If onion starts to burn, reduce heat.) Set aside.

Rinse quinoa with cold water until cool; drain. In a large mixing bowl, combine quinoa, onion, and remaining ingredients (except tomato). Mix well. Stir in tomato. Serve at room temperature.

Makes 8 servings

Helpful Hints

Quinoa must be rinsed well before cooking to remove a natural bitter-tasting but harmless coating. (The coating naturally protects quinoa from birds and insects.)

All ingredients except tomato can be prepared, combined, and chilled up to one day ahead. Add a small amount of broth if mixture seems dry, then stir in tomato.

VARIATION

Use a flavored oil to cook onion.

Per Serving:
143 Calories; 6g Protein; 4g Fat;
23g Carbohydrates; 0 Cholesterol;
75mg Sodium; 4g Fiber.

Tarragon-Barley Pilaf

1 cup uncooked quick-cooking
    barley
¼ cup chopped walnuts
2 shallots, finely chopped
    (about ¼ cup)
2 tablespoons tarragon-
    flavored white wine
    vinegar
1 tablespoon olive oil (optional)
½ teaspoon dried tarragon (or
    1 tablespoon finely chopped
    fresh tarragon)
¼ teaspoon salt
Freshly ground black pepper to
    taste

Prepare barley according to package directions. Drain, if necessary.

Meanwhile, toast walnuts in a dry skillet over medium-low heat, about 5 minutes, shaking pan frequently to prevent burning.

In a medium serving bowl, combine all remaining ingredients. Stir in barley and nuts. Serve warm.

Makes 4 servings

VARIATION

For a richer flavor, substitute vegetable broth for water when cooking barley.

Per Serving:
220 Calories; 4g Protein; 5g Fat; 41g Carbohydrates; 0 Cholesterol; 139mg Sodium; 6g Fiber.

CHAPTER 4

Desserts

Pumpkin Spice Muffins

1¾ **cups whole wheat pastry flour or unbleached white flour**
1 **teaspoon baking powder**
1 **teaspoon ground cinnamon**
½ **teaspoon baking soda**
¼ **teaspoon salt**
¾ **cup canned pumpkin**
⅔ **cup buttermilk**
½ **cup honey or rice syrup (see Helpful Hint)**
2 **egg whites, lightly beaten**
2 **tablespoons canola oil**

Preheat oven to 400°F. Line a 12-cup muffin pan with muffin papers.

In a large bowl, sift together flour, baking powder, cinnamon, baking soda, and salt. In a second bowl, stir together remaining ingredients. Add the pumpkin mixture to the flour mixture, stirring just until blended.

Divide batter equally among the 12 muffin cups. Bake until muffins are springy to the touch and lightly browned, about 20 minutes.

Makes 12 muffins

Helpful Hint

Rice syrup is a natural liquid sweetener made from brown rice. Its mild flavor is perfect when you don't want the distinct sweetness of white sugar or honey. Rice syrup is available in natural food stores.

Per Muffin:
136 Calories; 4g Protein; 3g Fat; 24g Carbohydratess; 1mg Cholesterol; 140mg Sodium; 3g Fiber.

Not-Too-Rich Brownies

Nonstick cooking spray
2 cups sugar
1¼ cups unbleached white flour
¾ cup unsweetened cocoa
¼ teaspoon salt
1 egg plus 1 egg white, beaten
1 teaspoon vanilla extract
½ cup melted reduced-fat
    margarine or butter
½ cup nonfat vanilla yogurt

Preheat oven to 350°F. Spray an 8-inch square baking pan with nonstick cooking spray; set aside.

Combine sugar, flour, cocoa, and salt in a mixing bowl. Make a well in the center; add beaten eggs and egg white and vanilla. Stir. Add margarine or butter and mix well. Stir in yogurt.

Spread mixture in prepared pan. Bake just until brownies begin to pull away from sides of pan, about 25 minutes. Cool before cutting into squares.

Makes sixteen 2-inch squares

Per Square:
187 Calories; 3g Protein; 5g Fat; 22g Carbohydrates; 11mg Cholesterol; 86mg Sodium; 2g Fiber.

Chocolate Chip Cookies

3 cups unbleached white flour
1 teaspoon baking soda
¾ cup unsweetened applesauce
¾ cup honey or rice syrup (see Helpful Hint)
2 teaspoons vanilla extract
¾ cup semisweet chocolate chips
½ cup chopped nuts or sunflower seeds (optional)

Preheat oven to 350°F.

In a large mixing bowl, combine flour and baking soda. In a second bowl, combine applesauce, honey or rice syrup, and vanilla. Add dry ingredients to wet ingredients. Stir in chocolate chips and nuts or sunflower seeds, if desired; mix well.

Drop cookie dough by teaspoonfuls onto a nonstick or lightly oiled cookie sheet. Flatten dough with fork. Bake until cookies are lightly browned, about 12 minutes. Remove cookies from cookie sheets immediately.

Makes about 4 dozen cookies

Helpful Hint

Rice syrup is a natural liquid sweetener made from brown rice. Its mild flavor is perfect when you don't want the distinct sweetness of white sugar or honey. Rice syrup is available in natural food stores.

Use more than one cookie sheet to make more cookies at the same time if your oven has the room. Be careful not to place one pan directly over another, though, and rotate pans from the top and bottom shelves halfway through the cooking time for even baking.

Per Cookie:
57 Calories; 1g Protein; 1g Fat; 6g Carbohydrates; 1mg Cholesterol; 18mg Sodium; 0 Fiber

Peanut Butter Snowballs

1 cup chopped nuts
1 cup raisins
1 cup nonfat dry milk or
    powdered soy milk (see
    Helpful Hint)
1 cup creamy peanut butter
1 cup honey or rice syrup
¼ cup wheat germ
1 cup unsweetened shredded
    coconut

In a large mixing bowl, combine all ingredients except coconut. Mix well. Shape mixture into 1-inch balls, then roll balls in coconut. (If mixture is too sticky to shape into balls, refrigerate until dough is firm enough to work with.)

Place balls on baking sheet lined with wax paper or plastic wrap and freeze. Serve frozen.

Makes about 5 dozen balls

Helpful Hints

Powdered soy milk is available in natural food stores.

Store balls in freezer in airtight container between layers of wax paper or plastic wrap.

Per Ball:
60 Calories; 2g Protein; 4g Fat;
4g Carbohydrates; 0 Cholesterol;
10mg Sodium; 1g Fiber.

Chocolate Ricotta Cream

One 15-ounce container part-
    skim ricotta cheese
5 tablespoons honey or rice
    syrup (see Helpful Hints)
2 tablespoons unsweetened
    cocoa
½ teaspoon vanilla extract
¼ teaspoon ground cinnamon
1 tablespoon sliced almonds,
    toasted (see Helpful Hints)

In a food processor or blender, process ricotta for 1 minute. Add honey or rice syrup, cocoa, vanilla, and cinnamon; process until smooth and creamy.

Spoon mixture into 6 dessert glasses. Garnish each serving with almonds.

Makes 6 servings

Helpful Hints

Rice syrup is a natural liquid sweetener made from brown rice. Its mild flavor is perfect when you don't want the distinct sweetness of white sugar or honey. Rice syrup is available in natural food stores.

To toast sliced almonds, place them in a dry skillet over medium-low heat. Cook until browned and fragrant, shaking skillet occasionally.

Per Serving:
144 Calories; 9g Protein; 5g Fat; 5g Carbohydrates; 22mg Cholesterol; 89mg Sodium; 1g Fiber.

Fresh Blackberry Pudding

4 cups apple juice
⅓ cup agar flakes (see Helpful Hints)
¼ cup honey or rice syrup, or to taste
1 tablespoon arrowroot powder (see Helpful Hints) or cornstarch
1 teaspoon fresh lemon juice
1 teaspoon vanilla extract
2 cups fresh blackberries

In a 2-quart saucepan, combine all ingredients except blackberries. Bring to a boil over medium-high heat. Reduce heat to medium; stir in blackberries.

Cook, stirring, for 1 minute. Remove from heat. Pour mixture into 8 serving dishes. Chill until firm.

Makes 8 servings

VARIATION

Substitute other fresh berries, such as raspberries, for blackberries.

Helpful Hints

Agar is a clear, flavorless sea vegetable that is freeze-dried, sold in sticks or flakes, and used like gelatin. It is also called agar-agar, and is available in natural food stores and some supermarkets.

Arrowroot is a powder derived from the arrowroot plant that is used as a thickener. Usually less processed than cornstarch, it can be substituted for it measure for measure. Arrowroot is sold in natural food stores and in some supermarkets.

Per Serving:
114 Calories; 0.2g Protein; 0.2g Fat; 28g Carbohydrates; 0 Cholesterol; 4mg Sodium; 2g Fiber.

Pears in Raspberry Sauce

3 firm Bosc or Bartlett pears
½ cup fresh orange juice
¼ cup raspberry jam or jelly
2 tablespoons mirin (see Helpful Hint), white wine, or fruit liqueur (optional)
Pinch ground cinnamon or nutmeg
Pinch salt
Fresh raspberries, strawberries, and mint leaves for garnish

Preheat oven to 350°F.

Cut pears in half lengthwise and scoop out seeds and core with a spoon. Place pears cut-side down in a baking dish.

Combine juice, jam or jelly, mirin, wine or liqueur, cinnamon or nutmeg, and salt. Pour over pears; cover dish with foil. Bake until pears are soft, about 25 minutes.

To serve, place pears cut-side up on serving dish, spoon sauce from baking dish over them, and garnish with berries and mint.

Makes 6 servings

Helpful Hint

Mirin is a sweet Japanese cooking wine made from rice that is sold in most supermarkets and natural food stores.

Per Serving:
98 Calories; 0.6g Protein; 0.5g Fat; 24g Carbohydrates; 0 Cholesterol; 46mg Sodium; 3g Fiber.

Warm Lime Bananas

A simple yet unique dessert redolent with Thai flavors.

4 fresh, firm bananas
1 tablespoon butter
3 to 4 tablespoons dark brown
   sugar or granulated sugar
   cane juice (see Helpful Hint)
Juice of 2 limes
Toasted coconut for garnish
   (optional)

Peel bananas and cut in half crosswise, then cut in half lengthwise. Set aside.

Melt butter in a large skillet over medium heat. Fry bananas until golden and slightly softened, about 5 minutes. Sprinkle sugar over top and continue cooking bananas, stirring occasionally, until sugar dissolves and becomes a syrup, about 4 minutes.

Arrange bananas on individual serving plates. Squeeze half a lime over each serving. Garnish with toasted coconut, if desired. Serve immediately.

Makes 4 servings

Helpful Hint

Granulated sugar cane juice is juice from the sugar cane plant that has been dried and granulated. It is used like white sugar and is sold in natural food stores.

Per Serving:
160 Calories; 1g Protein; 4g Fat; 35g Carbohydrates; 8mg Cholesterol; 34mg Sodium; 3g Fiber.

Layered Berry Parfaits

1 cup fresh blueberries
1 cup sliced fresh strawberries
1 cup fresh red currants
1 cup fresh blackberries
⅓ cup sweet dessert wine (such as sauterne) or apple juice
1½ cups fresh red raspberries
3 tablespoons maple syrup, or to taste
2 cups crumbled vanilla wafer cookies
4 sprigs fresh mint leaves

In a large bowl, combine blueberries, strawberries, currants, blackberries, and wine or apple juice. Let stand for 20 minutes, stirring occasionally. Meanwhile, puree raspberries and syrup in a blender or food processor until smooth.

To assemble dessert, spoon a layer of mixed berries into the bottom of 4 parfait glasses or wine glasses. Top with a drizzle of raspberry puree, then vanilla wafer crumbs. Repeat until all ingredients are used, ending with a drizzle of raspberry puree.

Garnish each serving with sprig of mint. If desired, chill parfaits for 1 hour before serving.

Makes 4 servings

VARIATION

Substitute any other fresh berries for those listed above.

Helpful Hint

You may substitute frozen berries for fresh, if desired, but frozen berries will exude more juice than fresh berries.

Per Serving:
329 Calories; 4g Protein; 4g Fat; 72g Carbohydrates; 2mg Cholesterol; 73mg Sodium; 9g Fiber.

Cranberry Cake

This lovely dessert has a layer of nuts and cranberries on the bottom and a cakelike "cobbler" top layer.

2 cups fresh or frozen
   cranberries
½ cup chopped walnuts or
   pecans
1½ cups sugar, divided
1 cup unbleached white flour
½ cup nonfat plain or vanilla
   yogurt cheese (see Helpful
   Hints, page 13)
⅓ cup butter, melted and
   cooled
2 eggs
¼ teaspoon salt
¼ teaspoon almond extract
Vanilla ice cream (optional)

Preheat oven to 350°F.

Combine cranberries, nuts and ½ cup sugar in a 9 x 13-inch baking pan that has been sprayed with nonstick cooking spray. Spread mixture evenly in pan. Set aside.

In a medium bowl, combine remaining 1 cup sugar and remaining ingredients. Stir with whisk until batter is smooth. Pour batter over cranberries; spread evenly.

Bake until cake tester inserted in center comes out clean, about 25 minutes. Serve warm with vanilla ice cream if desired.

Makes 12 servings

Per Serving:
141 Calories; 4g Protein; 9g Fat; 12g Carbohydrates; 41mg Cholesterol; 123mg Sodium; 1g Fiber.

Sautéed Apple Topping

¼ cup apple cider or apple juice
1 tablespoon brown sugar
1 tablespoon butter
¼ teaspoon ground cinnamon
2 medium tart apples, cored,
 quartered lengthwise and
 sliced crosswise
1 to 2 teaspoons finely chopped
 crystallized ginger
1 teaspoon cornstarch mixed
 with 1 teaspoon cold water

In a 3-quart saucepan, combine cider or juice, sugar, butter, and cinnamon. Bring to a boil over medium heat. Stir in apples and ginger. Simmer until apples are tender, about 8 minutes, gently stirring occasionally.

Add cornstarch mixture; stir just until liquid is thickened and glossy. Serve apple topping over ice cream, shortcake biscuits, or gingerbread.

Makes about 2 cups; 6 servings

VARIATION

Add ½ cup raisins to saucepan with apples.

For a lovely holiday dish, add about 2 tablespoons milk, soy milk, or cream and serve over mashed sweet potatoes.

Per ⅓ Cup:
56 Calories; 1g Protein; 2g Fat; 10g Carbohydrates; 5mg Cholesterol; 21mg Sodium; 1g Fiber.

Creamy Tofu Pudding

This is as close to instant vanilla pudding as you can get without the box, and is a classic recipe for people who avoid dairy-based dishes.

One 10½-ounce package firm
  tofu, chilled, cubed
¼ cup honey or rice syrup (see
  Helpful Hint)
½ teaspoon vanilla extract
⅛ teaspoon ground cinnamon
Chopped fresh or dried fruit
  (optional)

Combine tofu, honey or rice syrup, vanilla, and cinnamon in a blender or food processor. Process until smooth. Top each serving with fruit, if desired.

Makes 1⅓ cups; 2 servings

VARIATIONS

Add your favorite ripe fruit to the blender or food processor to make fruit pudding.

For chocolate pudding, prepare as directed above, omitting cinnamon. Add 2 tablespoons unsweetened cocoa. If desired, add ¼ teaspoon almond extract and top with chopped nuts or miniature chocolate chips.

Helpful Hint

Rice syrup is a natural liquid sweetener made from brown rice. Its mild flavor is perfect when you don't want the distinct sweetness of white sugar or honey. Rice syrup is available in natural food stores.

Per Serving:
220 Calories; 10g Protein; 4g Fat;
39g Carbohydrates; 0 Cholesterol;
52mg Sodium; 2g Fiber.

Fantastic Vanilla Pudding

2 cups 1-percent milk
3 tablespoons cornstarch
3 tablespoons maple syrup
⅛ teaspoon salt
1 teaspoon vanilla extract

In a 1½-quart saucepan, combine all ingredients except vanilla; stir well to eliminate lumps. Heat over medium heat until mixture boils, about 7 minutes; boil for 1 minute, stirring constantly. Stir in vanilla.

Spoon pudding into individual serving dishes. Serve warm or cold.

**Makes 2 cups;
four ½-cup servings**

VARIATION

For chocolate pudding, stir in ¼ cup semisweet chocolate chips after mixture comes to a boil.

Per ½ Cup:
115 Calories; 4g Protein; 2g Fat;
22g Carbohydrates; 5mg Cholesterol; 130mg Sodium; <1g Fiber.

Chewy Whole Grain Cereal Bars

Nonstick cooking spray
½ cup honey or rice syrup (see Helpful Hints)
½ cup chunky almond butter or peanut butter
½ cup nonfat dry milk powder or soy milk powder (see Helpful Hints)
3 cups whole grain flake cereal
1 cup dried fruit bits

Spray an 8-inch square baking dish with nonstick cooking spray. Set aside.

In a 3-quart saucepan, combine honey or rice syrup and almond butter or peanut butter. Heat over medium heat until melted and smooth, about 2 minutes, stirring constantly. Stir in milk powder or soy milk powder until blended.

Add cereal and fruit bits; stir until coated. Spoon mixture into prepared dish; spread evenly and press into dish with back of spoon. Serve immediately, or refrigerate until firm. (Bars are easier to slice when firm.)

Makes 16 bars

Helpful Hint

Rice syrup is a natural liquid sweetener made from brown rice. Its mild flavor is perfect when you don't want the distinct sweetness of white sugar or honey. Rice syrup is available in natural food stores.

Soy milk powder is available in natural food stores.

Per Bar:
154 Calories; 6g Protein; 5g Fat; 25g Carbohydrates; 1mg Cholesterol; 171mg Sodium; 6g Fiber.

Sliced Pear Sauté with Almonds

This dessert is flavorful and elegant, but simple enough to make on any occasion.

4 medium pears, cored and cut lengthwise into ¼-inch slices
3 tablespoons fresh lemon juice
1 teaspoon canola oil
½ cup fresh orange juice
¼ cup sliced almonds
¼ cup honey
1 to 1½ teaspoons grated orange peel
1 teaspoon almond extract
½ teaspoon ground cinnamon

Place pear slices in a large non-stick skillet. Sprinkle slices with lemon juice and oil; toss lightly to coat. Cook over medium-high heat, stirring pear slices constantly, until hot, about 2 minutes. Cover, reduce heat to medium-low, and simmer until pears are tender, about 4 minutes.

Remove pears from skillet using a slotted spoon, and divide evenly into serving dishes. Set aside.

Add remaining ingredients to skillet. Cook, stirring constantly, over medium-high heat until syrupy, about 3 minutes. Spoon sauce evenly over pears.

Makes 4 to 6 servings

Per Serving:
236 Calories; 2g Protein; 6g Fat; 48g Carbohydrates; 0 Cholesterol; 2mg Sodium; 5g Fiber.

Rhubarb-Strawberry Sauce

This fresh-tasting ice cream topping is a perfect way to welcome the first fruits of spring.

3 cups chopped fresh rhubarb
½ cup sugar
½ cup fresh orange juice
1 teaspoon grated orange peel
¼ teaspoon almond extract
1 teaspoon cornstarch mixed
**   with 1 tablespoon water**
2 cups sliced fresh strawberries

In a 1½-quart saucepan, combine rhubarb, sugar, orange juice, orange peel, and almond extract. Cook over medium-high heat, stirring frequently, just until rhubarb is tender, about 5 minutes.

Stir in cornstarch-water mixture. Cook, stirring constantly, until sauce is thickened, about 1 minute. Remove from heat. Stir in strawberries. Serve warm over vanilla or cinnamon ice cream.

Makes 2¾ cups;
about 5 servings

Per ½ Cup Serving:
107 Calories; 0.9g Protein; 0.9g Fat; 26g Carbohydrates; 0 Cholesterol; 4mg Sodium; 2g Fiber.

Cherries and Chocolate Dumplings

¾ **cup unbleached white flour**
¾ **cup sugar**
¼ **cup unsweetened cocoa**
1½ **teaspoons baking powder**
¼ **teaspoon salt**
3 **tablespoons butter**
¼ **cup skim milk**
1 **egg**
One 20-ounce package frozen dark sweet cherries, thawed
½ **cup water**
2 **teaspoons cornstarch mixed with 2 tablespoons water**

In a medium mixing bowl, combine flour, ¼ cup sugar, cocoa, baking powder, and salt. Cut butter into flour mixture with a fork or pastry blender until mixture resembles coarse crumbs.

In a 1-cup measure or small bowl, combine milk and egg; mix well. Stir milk mixture into flour just until moistened; set aside.

In a large skillet, combine cherries, remaining ½ cup sugar, and water. Bring to a simmer over medium-high heat, stirring occasionally. Stir in cornstarch-water mixture. Cook, stirring constantly, until sauce is thickened, about 1 minute.

Reduce heat to low. Drop dumpling mixture by heaping tablespoonfuls into hot cherry sauce. Cover and simmer until dumplings are cooked through, about 10 minutes. Serve immediately.

Makes 5 to 6 servings

VARIATION

Serve dessert with a scoop of vanilla ice cream or nonfat frozen yogurt.

Per Serving:
325 Calories; 6g Protein; 9g Fat; 60g Carbohydrates; 51mg Cholesterol; 345mg Sodium; 3g Fiber.

Fruit-Nut Balls

1½ **cups mixed dried fruit bits**
⅔ **cup sugar**
1 egg
2 egg whites
¾ **cup finely chopped walnuts**
    or pecans
1 teaspoon vanilla extract
Additional sugar for coating

In a 2-quart saucepan, combine fruit, sugar, egg, and egg whites; mix well. Cook over low heat, stirring constantly, until mixture thickens and pulls away from side of pan, about 10 minutes.

Remove from heat. Stir in nuts and vanilla. Place pan in a large bowl filled with water and ice cubes, and stir mixture until it is cool enough to handle, about 3 minutes.

Shape mixture into 1- or 1½-inch balls. Roll balls in additional sugar. Serve. Store balls in refrigerator in an airtight container that has been lined with wax paper.

**Makes about
2 dozen 1½-inch balls or about
3 dozen 1-inch balls.**

Per Ball:
72 Calories; 1g Protein; 2g Fat;
12g Carbohydrates; 7mg Cholesterol; 9mg Sodium; 0.9g Fiber.

Apricot-Date Dessert

This flavorful dessert is best served warm with a scoop of vanilla ice cream or frozen yogurt.

2 tablespoons butter
½ cup uncooked old-fashioned oats
¼ cup packed brown sugar
3 tablespoons unbleached white flour
One 6-ounce package dried apricots
½ cup chopped dried dates
½ cup fresh orange juice
Vanilla ice cream (optional)

Preheat oven to 400°F.

Place butter in an 8-inch square baking dish. Place baking dish in oven and melt butter; remove from oven.

Stir oats, sugar, and flour into melted butter; mix well. Bake mixture until oats are toasted, about 12 minutes, stirring mixture twice while baking.

While oat mixture is baking, combine apricots, dates, and orange juice in a 1-quart saucepan. Cook over medium heat until mixture boils and thickens, about 8 minutes, stirring frequently. Remove from heat. Place pan in a large bowl of ice water, and stir mixture until it is slightly cooled, about 5 minutes.

Remove ⅓ of oatmeal mixture from baking dish and set aside. Press remaining oatmeal evenly on bottom of pan. Spoon apricots and dates evenly over crust, spreading carefully. Sprinkle with reserved oatmeal. Serve warm with ice cream.

Makes 9 servings

Per Serving:
142 Calories; 2g Protein; 3g Fat; 28g Carbohydrates; 7mg Cholesterol; 31mg Sodium; 3g Fiber.

Broiled Berry Dessert

5 cups mixed berries, fresh or frozen (thawed)
2 teaspoons grated fresh orange peel
1 cup nonfat or low-fat plain yogurt
¼ teaspoon ground cinnamon
¼ cup brown sugar

Preheat broiler.

In a medium bowl, combine berries and orange peel. In a small bowl, combine yogurt and cinnamon.

Divide berries equally among 4 individual gratin or other oven-proof dishes. Top evenly with yogurt. Sprinkle 1 tablespoon brown sugar over each.

Broil about 5 inches from heat until sugar melts and caramelizes, about 4 minutes. Serve immediately.

Makes 4 servings

VARIATION

Sprinkle berry mixture with orange-flavored liqueur before dividing into dishes.

Per Serving:
147 Calories; 5g Protein; 1g Fat; 33g Carbohydrates; 1mg Cholesterol; 57mg Sodium; 6g Fiber.